THE SHAPE OF FURTHER THINGS

THE SHAPE OF FURTHER THINGS

SPECULATIONS ON CHANGE

Brian W. Aldiss

With appendices by Dr. Christopher Evans and others

FABER & FABER · London

First published in 1970
by Faber and Faber Limited
24 Russell Square London WC1
Printed in Great Britain by
Latimer Trend & Co Ltd Plymouth
All rights reserved

ISBN 0 571 09472 4

Half our lives we pass in the shadow of Earth, and the brother of death exacteth a third part of our lives. A good part of our sleep is peered out with visions and fantastical objects, wherein we are confessedly deceived.

Sir Thomas Browne On Dreams

We need a different language for every patient.

Carl Jung
Memories, Dreams, Reflections

Contents

9

Contents

The article quoted on pages 160–164 is reprinted by kind
permission of the Editor of *The Guardian*

Introduction

Earth is charged with a beauty we are destroying because we ourselves are charged with a beauty rarely released. Such, you might say, is the pole about which these speculations revolve. We are infinitely rich, yet we mess about with penny-in-the-slot machines.

The speculations concern themselves with processes going on inside and outside the human skull. These processes are changing and interacting.

As dynastic Chinese worshipped their ancestors, so the present dynasties of the West are inclining towards descendant-worship. We imagine we have thrown away the past only because the burden of the future grows heavier. Rightly, we begin to fear about the sort of world we are bequeathing our grandsons.

Such care for the future must be fostered, and seen as a challenge rather than a threat. This is because the future in any practical sense always refuses to exist; all that lies ahead is our image of the future, which means our collective image of how our collective actions are going to work out.

We have more power, more information, than ever before; how is it our collective actions are not working out very well? Should we perhaps turn that power and information to working our own selves out? The future might then look a little less bloodshot than it does.

Speculation about change includes a consideration of the sub-literature of change, science-fiction. Men like H. G. Wells and Guillaume Apollinaire invented this treacherous medium in which I work myself. It is an important medium, at least potentially, and so I have included among my speculations fragments from its incestuous recent history.

My main concern, however, is more presumptuous. Entering

my subject through a study of dreams—those spores of thought as transient yet enduring as pollen—I go on to discuss how we might deal with some of our inadequacies and unleash some of our potentialities almost immediately. Although there is no doubt that the human (or let's more modestly say the European) psyche could explosively improve its condition, the improvement has to come soon, before the ever-self-renewing battalions of technology overwhelm us; sardines in the tin take no pride in canning industries or marketing research.

This whole subject is of such importance that perhaps an amateur thinker may be allowed his say.

Since speculations in thin air, even on thick subjects, are insipid fare, I have set them within the period and environment in which the book was written. Grass was growing outside as the pages came off the typewriter; my hope is that readers may find the pages more tolerable for the reminder of grass. Letters from friends and ringing phones punctuate discussions on the nature of the brain that invented those instruments of communication; domestic affairs counterbalance theory. Maybe the result has a curious charm.

To retain this effect, I have resisted the impulse to edit out facts and anticipations while revising. I wanted to preserve the sandwich as it was, even at the risk of curling edges. Some of the personal projects mentioned in passing turned out in ways entirely other than anticipated (for one instance, my novel, *The Hand-Reared Boy*, met some difficulties, and in fact will appear from a publisher other than the one named), while others matured in ways beyond anticipation (our daughter Charlotte, *in utero* while the book was being written, is more delightful than we had any right to guess).

These simple ways in which I was unable to foresee simple events even two months ahead should give readers ample warning of my—and anyone's—fallibility when turning to predict large and complex events two decades ahead. The future, even more than the past, is built in our own image. Other people's images keep getting in the way.

My debts in this book are many; I try to acknowledge most of them as I go along. But I have to thank in particular Dr. Christopher Evans for allowing me to quote from and include articles written by him and his colleagues; they are reproduced by permission of the Director of the National Physical Laboratory. This book owes its inspiration to a conversation Dr. Evans and I enjoyed one winter evening.

BRIAN W. ALDISS

Heath House
Southmoor
May 1969

1 A Fantastic Vision After Midnight

Fifteen minutes into Thursday, 9th January 1969. I've been walking up and down my drive by the light of a half-moon, low in the east, over Oxford, over East Anglia, over the North German plain, over Russia, over the slow-grinding globe. The drive, about a hundred yards of it, is fringed by lime and beech trees. Their shadows were long in the moonlight.

Long and entangled, like the terminator between Time Present and Time Future.

My location: a little village called Southmoor, in Berkshire, England. Time and place are important. Relatively important. Important in the ticking mechanism of my mind. Margaret, heavy with child, goes to bed; I come up here to my study to write—a decision I took in the drive while pacing up and down among the cool shadows.

As I did my walking, the ticking was as loud and clear as the moon. Thought. A separate thing, altogether removed from the ancestor-invoking silence of night. My body carried it effortlessly up and down, up and down. What that body of thought was, I will try to tell here. First, get the simple thing right—habitat, the old human thing: man married to his local acre. I'm married to my local acre, though in fact we have lived in this place for only half a year. We may stay here for the rest of our lives. It is intensely dear to me—I own Heath House in the way that the moon and tree shadows own me: by falling across me and influencing me intensely. As I swing restlessly northwards up the drive, I see the house. Some lights still burning. Otherwise a black outline, square, uncompromising. Built by a Baptist missionary in 1837, a righteous man who came to bring the light to this hamlet over a century ago. He left his mark on the territory if not the minds, building the local chapel as well as this house.

The house is black through the trees, against the deepest blue of the sky. Uncompromising, as I say. Only when you get close do you discern—dimly in the moonlight cast across the face of the house—that a later minister, more relaxed, more Victorian than the first incumbent, built on to the original slate-roofed pencil-box a gloriously pretentious porch, with four columns of the Corinthian order. And a fine bay window. And an ample conservatoire, which later collapsed and has now disappeared, though its ground plan remains in the form of black-and-red tiles outside the dining-room window. This is my house. *Pro tem.*

It became my house—half of it is Margaret's—through my will and our intention. We could not afford it, but we bought it. You have already met two of the most compelling reasons why we bought it. The drive, and the schizophrenic front of the house: whose severe and rigorous outline melts into a certain robust *luxuria* as you draw nearer. I recognized a physical analogue of my own character when I saw it.

But my pacing. My pacing after bedtime. After all, I am forty-three, and have at last taken to going to bed regularly and early, since our marriage three years ago. For the pleasure and profit of it.

Friends of ours have just left. Dr. Christopher Evans and his wife Nancy. They came down from Twickenham for drinks, dinner, and talk. And after we had waved goodbye to them from the Corinthian porch, my brain remained at high pitch, churning over what we had said and had not managed to say.

Haven't you ever thought to yourself after a pleasant evening—or even after a dull afternoon—that if you could but have it all again, preferably in slow motion, then you could trace in it all the varied strands of your life? Haven't you ever thought, on certain beautiful and privileged days of your life (and the dull days are privileged too), that they contain all those varied strands?—And that the fact that certain finite strands of time, like our evening tonight, could contain all those strands is an incredible wealth, rather than a poverty?

Isn't wealth in life to be accounted as much in its condensation as its dispersal? I see the answer to my rhetorical question is no, for I have phrased it wrongly. Put it this way. Life needs diversity; the more the better; but the diversity only acquires value if it can occasionally be glimpsed through the magnifying lens of an evening, or of the sort of brief span of time that a mind can hold conveniently in the metaphorical palm of its hand.

This feeling has often come over me. For once I will put it to the test. I will explore some of the strands of what, after all, is only a fairly representative evening. (I have often talked longer, and to closer friends, and drunk more!) Does this mean I am embarking—oh God, not that!—on a whole book? Time now: Zero zero forty-three. The time-terminator moving with elaborate ease.

That perfect silence. The sheer delight of being alive. The constant surprise of each day. I never seem to run out of astonishment. It would be tremendous to try and capture in a book the particular astonishment of living now: at the end of the sixties, the beginning of the seventies.

Every time has its particular flavour. In political Europe, a stalemate of manœuvrability seems to have set in. On the one hand, the earlier promise of economic union has been denied; on the other, room for genuine statesmanly initiative is limited while the two super-powers maintain their deadly balance of power. Yet, for all that, one detects an undercurrent of excitement in Europe, an expectation, as if, given a day of sunshine, new green shoots would burst through the forest floor. This is nowhere more true than in Britain, where a mood of determined euphoria had persisted through all the economic crises of the last few years. It is as if people were deliberately dissociating themselves from their governments.

Looking more widely, we see another excitement is abroad: the excitement of the serial civilization, for ever promising more thrills tomorrow. To maintain our stands of living, we may not stand still. We live in Red Queen's country—'it takes all the running you can do to stay in the same place. If you want to get somewhere else, you must run at least twice as fast as that!'

We are running twice as fast. The Anglo-French Concorde will soon be rupturing the air; jumbo jets will land us in tourist-saturated resorts; our streets will be chocked with double the number of automobiles. But of course we shall adapt—after a fashion. Even if some of the quality of life will be lost.

If I am writing a book, then that must be its overriding subject and its final topic: the precious quality of life. It was one of the assumptions behind our talk tonight, that life is rich and sweet and battle must be joined to keep it that way. What an irony it is that, just at a time when more people than ever are escaping from the serfdom of life to savour the good things, everything should be growing more organized, more automatic, the juices squeezed out between the millstones of runaway technology and runaway population!

If our conversation had a main theme, it was the research on which Chris is involved, about which I shall have more to say later. At the moment, it's sufficient to say that we were discussing his theory of dreaming which treats the brain as a functioning entity similar in effect to the computer; and that this theory is immensely of the present day, since it couples hard and soft science, since it couples man and machine. Our debate also roved round marginal points; for both of us, these marginal points were the gravy of the joint.

For we were asking, implicitly, What is the brain? And thus, What is man? And thus, Where is he going? And we discovered that we had been thinking about this question for a number of years. Since our childhood, in fact. And this is what this book will also have to be about. It was not just what Chris and Nancy said. It was also what we didn't say: for in my case, behind everything lay my reservations—not so much about science, but about the role that scientists and their base-wallahs and their salesmen are forcing science, or more particularly technology, to play in our lives.

Events do not move towards benevolent ends. We grow increasingly aware of the way in which our natural environment is becoming polluted, ruined, and destroyed: not only by monstrous larval flows of concrete over green land (such as threatens Heath House on its own tiny scale) but by the chemicals with complex artificial molecules—D.D.T. is the best-known example—which are not broken down easily by the forces of nature.

As our external environment is becoming polluted, so our minds may undergo a similar process. Human attitudes cannot remain the same in a changing world. As the globe becomes crammed with people, an ever-increasing proportion of whom will be under-nourished, under-privileged, and sub-normal in intelligence as a result of congenital malnutrition, will not even the image of motherhood, hitherto so sacred to us, become a symbol of destruction?

We have to learn to live with the advantages we have, to retain any advantages at all. And for most of us, that means we must be taught to live. Western man has achieved his staggering technological success by maiming himself; in our schools and universities, we are instructed in matters that will assist 'our' careers so that, in effect, we can further the imperialisms of 'our' society. We are not instructed in what we are, or in how we can become ourselves more fully, or in how we may best understand ourselves and, through ourselves, others.

As I see it, this extraordinary lacuna must be filled soon if humans are to retain their foothold in humanity.

Anything that contributes, therefore, to knowledge of ourselves is to the general good. At present, we have tantalizing new glimpses of how our brains work. Chris Evans and his colleagues provide one. The hallucinogenic drugs such as LSD provide us with others. Much more research is needed in these areas.

Manuals are available on the working and maintenance of almost any make of car. But try and find a straightforward manual that summarizes present knowledge of the working and maintenance of the brain! There isn't one, as far as I have been able to discover.

It is perhaps part of the western success/disaster story that many people are terrified of what they may find in their own brains. They imagine that countless old horror films lie somewhere inside the cerebral vaults, ready to launch on their discoverer a teeming quota of Draculas and Frankensteins. Certainly the territories of the mind are a domain of magic, as all art reports; awe awaits there but not terror; animality but not degradation; and we should not fear them. The same applies when the filters of sleep obscure those territories. Sir Thomas Browne had the right attitude on this as on many things when he began his famous essay *On Dreams* with that sonorous passage: 'Half our lives we pass in the shadow of Earth, and the brother of Death exacteth a third part of our lives. . . . A good part of our sleep is peered out with visions and fantastical objects, wherein we are confessedly deceived.'

Our educational systems should contain more fantastical visions and fewer sliderules.

Another passage from Browne is worth quoting here. It occurs in his *Letter to a Friend*, an account of the passing of a mutual friend, in which stands a beautiful paragraph beginning, 'He was now past the healthful Dreams of the Sun, Moon and Stars, in their Clarity and proper Courses. 'Twas too late to dream of Flying, of Limpid Fountains, smooth Waters, white Vestments, and fruitful green Trees, which are the Visions of healthful Sleeps, and at good Distance from the Grave.'

These passages I read to Chris. They have a beauty that supplements any argument. And Browne remains relevant today. A mid-seventeenth-century man, a general practitioner of Norwich —until the Black Death England's second city—he stood between the medieval and the modern, partly subscribing to Galen's and, though Galen, Hippocrates' received ideas—partly trying to think and observe for himself—but not entirely succeeding. The modern analogies are clear. We also only partly succeed. But what is the post-modern, the future, thinking towards which we work? This was also a subject of our talk this evening.

I mentioned to Chris the curious essay by the German Von Kleist on the way ideas are spontaneously generated in conversation. We generated ideas tonight. It's a common experience. And it's a common experience that I want to pin down here. To give to people who believe that the future is something more than a period in history, like, say, the Victorian Age.

Chris talked a great deal about the nature of words. He spoke of the reverence that primitive people have for words. Being averse to the idea of telepathy, he was talking of the way in which words have to be painfully formulated, and how, in our processes of selection of them, we have to slow down our thinking, and impoverish it, and dilute the whole business of mind-to-mind communication: so that speech can never have superseded telepathy, because even a primitive form of telepathy would have such great directness that the labour of speech could never provide a substitute for it.

But computers will so speed communications between each other that they will achieve the equivalent of telepathy.

He was saying how much and how fast computers have developed. How this speed goes almost unobserved—unobserved both by the general public and by the technicians working on computers; because both these classes are too near to or too far from the subject to have the proper perspective, just as the growth of a plant is more observable by the weekend gardener than by a real daily man or a casual visitor to the garden. He (and, he courteously implied, I) could see this speedy growth, being inter-disciplinary men. We began to indulge in conjecture on this theme, to build a simple partial diagram of the future.

Chris said, 'At the National Physical Laboratory where I work, I'm a subscriber to Telcomp, which links me to a computer a few miles away. You could get the G.P.O. to put you on the circuit too, if you wanted, although it's pretty costly as yet. You get a separate telephone and a switch-box, and can just dial yourself on to the computer. It comes through on a sort of telex machine not much bigger than an ordinary typewriter, and talks to you in almost ordinary English.

'This is the area where some of the major advances are now coming—the software is being radically simplified. Soon you'll be able to talk to computers practically man-to-man.

'You must come over and play with this computer some time.'

We talked about the increase of knowledge and information, together with the parallel increase in its availability. That availability has to increase immeasurably. In a few of my stories, I have written about wrist-computers, computers of perhaps limited abilities that—thanks to increasing micro-miniaturization processes—can be strapped to the wrist like watches. Talking to Chris Evans, I saw this was a mistaken idea. Link-ups between big computers are perhaps only a matter of time. Computer spin-off is piling up: fast-reading machines are coming on to the market, mass-production of cheap memories is on its way. Soon, soon, the contents of antiquated knowledge-repositories like the British Museum Reading Room can be transferred to computers. Imagine the jump in potential when that store of knowledge alone is available to a dialling subscriber. When that and similar information-system-nuclei are really available at the fingertips . . . the possessors of those fingertips will be living virtually in a different kind of environment, an environment with a lushness which will make ours seem like a desert with a few antique temples standing crumbling here and there.

What one will then wear on the wrist will be, not a mini-computer, but a computerized dialling system to the big hook-up.

The implications of this are almost limitless. The nature of learning is going to have to change; in a world where all the facts of a culture are at one's fingertips, education must transform itself.

Curiously enough, what is perhaps the first inkling of newer educational systems is now coming through. Britain's first—and the world's most far-reaching—Open University goes on the air soon with TV courses with elaborate soft-ware backing. It will be turning out its first B.A.s in 1974. A freeing of knowledge by mass-communication, a move at last against the segregation of facts in monasteries, universities and colleges—even though a final screening-through-examination will be retained.

While Chris and I were talking about these transformations, we were not alone. You should have the scene. The exterior of Heath House by moonlight you have pictured; now come inside. Please be welcome.

From the pretentious porch, you enter the front hall. The dining-room is on your right, the living-room on your left. We have dined on the right; now we are sitting comfortably in the room on the left, round a log fire. Apart from my fine cat, Nickie, those present are Chris and I and our two wives and Margaret's mother. Mama is living with us until her bungalow becomes available. The ladies have been talking about children, their own particular bit of the future under their charge. When they hear what we are saying about education, the two conversations merge.

'But a formal education is surely very good for a child's mind,' says Mama, who was a teacher. 'It isn't merely a stuffing with facts but a structure that teaches a child to think.'

We are in agreement with this, but I add, 'Despite that, it is *also* a stuffing with facts; and to a child it often appears merely a stuffing with facts.'

'And much Victorian education was just a cram,' Margaret points out. 'Today's better education has only slightly grown out of its old ways.'

'Quite so. And hasn't been able to throw off its origins. You still need to fill the child's brain with details about the wheat production of Canada and the strange affair of the square on the hypotenuse. But in future that need won't exist. Facts won't be stored inefficiently in privileged heads; they'll be the inheritance of every man, like the franchise. On your wrist—or maybe round your knee if man is going to become a more sedentary animal and mini-trousers arrive!—you will have an instrument that can tee you in immediately to a central computer which will provide whatever facts you require.'

'Exactly,' said Chris, 'except that "immediately" may not be the right word, since the whole operation will probably come under the province of the G.P.O.'

We laugh.

We decided that what is required is a Communications Company, under which telephonic and radiophonic channels will be integrated. But Chris's small reservation—'immediately may not be the right word'—symbolizes something important when trying to visualize the future, something I generally attempt to represent in my own fiction: when new things arrive, they function without attaining perfection; and even their long continuance may not bring them nearer to perfection, since other factors in that continuance militate against it. One example, before we return to the conversation.

Let's take the G.P.O. already mentioned.

The ordinary telephone, although its design is backward compared with the beautiful handpieces used by Swedish subscribers, is a pleasant-looking and efficient instrument. It will be more efficient when a vision-screen is added, and that in turn will also be more efficient when developments in holography allow a 3-D image (though it could be that the G.P.O. might drag its feet long enough to come right out with a 3-D screen straight off). But the system *behind* the handset is not merely an object, a technological still-life, but an organization, and organizations are always subject to stresses and strains. So that, perfect though your phone may be, it may take you ten minutes and a couple of wrong numbers before you speak to a subscriber ten miles away.

Why haven't the G.P.O. engineers got the system to rights by now? Because the system will not hold still, items obsolesce, relays fail, the number of subscribers grows—the G.P.O. is a physical embodiment of T. S. Eliot's line about 'a raid on the inarticulate With shabby equipment always deteriorating'. . . .

So it will be, I'd bet, with the CCDC (Computer Centre Dial Control). Perhaps I'm merely being guilty of an ingrained British suspicion of big organizations when I say that it is in the largest organizations the largest inefficiencies occur; chaos is a constant factor of systems. Suppose that, in the year 2002, a chap in Newcastle-upon-Tyne wants information about coproliths which he knows is held in the Smithsonian Institute in Washington D.C. He punches an eleven-digit number on his 'ward' (as the instrument on his wrist is commonly called by analogy with 'watch') and so is connected by radio and cable with the computer centre in London. He asks for the information. The computer keeps the line open while it communicates through its own ultra-rapid channels with the Smithsonian computer. The information comes back, and is given in English to the subscriber in Newcastle.

Alternatively, depending on how elaborate the in-coming information is, he may get it in visual form from over a TV-attachment in his home, or both, or in printed form over the same teletype that delivers his letters and his newspaper. Whatever the method, his wait is negligible.

Thus, things always work in science-fiction stories! Perfectly! But think of the discrepancies that might creep in on even such a simple operation in real life, the times the subscriber may be cut off in mid-sentence or mid-pause! Nor is it everyone who can dial an eleven-digit number with facility. Organization comes between people and things, just as it comes between people and people.

Despite the malfunctions of the system, however, the ward will be able to furnish you with just about any information you require.

Mama said, 'I still wonder what will happen if formal education disappears.'

'We can't tell,' I said, 'but at least you can be sure there will be no vacuum. What I imagine will happen is that education will be completely overhauled. You know that I'm generally accounted a pessimist, simply because I don't see that the basic human condition has radically improved over the centuries—

though I'd grant you an exception as far as dentistry and allied fields are concerned—but on this issue I'm very optimistic.

'Can you imagine the radical changes in human thought and feeling that might come about if the educational system were allowed to take children between the ages of, say, five and fifteen —just ten years—and teach them patterns of thought and behaviour which would help them not to pass exams but to live happily and sanely?—Give them an education in living rather than job-grabbing?'

2 The Education of H. G. Wells

I get this far and my vision fails. It is almost three o'clock in the morning. 9th January. I put out the light and stare through the study window. My eyes lose their flowers and bars and wounds of light; reality blossoms outside, lit by the moon, the incredible random patterns of reality. Moonlight still slants across the drive and the field. I can see one of the horses standing there, under the clump of Scots pines. Is the horse sleeping? Chris should measure its eye movements.

Something benevolent is generated in my mind, possibly because I am looking at a still picture that is not still, like a Warhol movie, restful for the eye-movements if somewhat numbing for the brain. At this moment, standing relaxed at the window, I am indulging in a sensuous secret connection, connected to infinitudes of experience that stand outside the frame of time: experience beyond analysis, at whose origins we can scarcely glance. My mind is open wide, as the iris of Nickie's eye will be at this hour.

Only simple and symbolic things confront me. That very moon, though in an earlier phase, was orbited by astronauts for the first time over the Christmas just gone; they left no more trace in the heavens than a wound in water; nevertheless, my brain retains their still trajectory. Their voyage is a mark in the mind. Moonlit nights are different from now on, framed with fatidical powers.

All things are in union. I go reluctantly to bed.

Next morning begins with the jolly calls of Timothy, now almost eighteen months old. In ten weeks, he will have a new brother or sister. He is Margaret's first-born, and my third child, a dear and happy creature, full of humour and energy, intelligent and therefore cautious, highly observant, madly talkative, just starting to communicate by speech. He communicates his good spirits to me, although I also am cheerful, being full of the book I so rashly began the night before.

Downstairs, the ruins of the meal we ate with the Evanses greet us. Some of the fine beef bourguignon remains. The wine's all gone, and Margaret and I scoffed the last of the flan at midnight, after the guests had departed.

We breakfast cosily in the kitchen. Leaving the debris to Margaret and Mama, I come upstairs and am writing again by ten o'clock. Fog outside, and frost on the tufts of grass. The mood of the weather has changed completely since three o'clock this morning.

My mood remains the same. I'm filled with the sense that last night encapsulated many of the important trends of my life, and of my response to science and speculation. I remember the feeling before; it came over me strongly in the Continental Hotel in Oslo, over a year ago, standing in that beautiful hotel room and wishing I could capture the thing entire.

> . . . Would we not shatter it and then
> Remould it nearer to the heart's desire?

No! To remould would be to shatter. The revelation has to come over at once in its untidiness and its total relevance.

Presumably this is one thing that a proper education in the future might be able to do. It would strengthen the mind's power to hold thought. Chris was talking last night about the way ignorant people use words as if they were bricks, behind which they proceed to build themselves a wall; whereas words are—what did he say they were? I've forgotten! Something tremulous and fluid, far removed from a Fletton! But the educated also fall

into category troubles. I have seen the way writer-friends of mine
have been pushed into categories by journalists, to their detri-
ment; Kingsley Amis (my own generation) suffered for a number
of years from the Angry Young Man label. I suffer from the
label 'science fiction writer', which allows the *Times Literary
Supplement* to toss one of my speculative novels, *Report on
Probability A*, to a hard-core SF man, who savages it for not being
hard-core SF! But under a proper education for living, such desperate needs to pigeonhole things would disappear. Life fades on
the stem when it is classified: the life of the spirit, I mean.

'Only connect!' All things connect, all things are holophrastic.
Education in future must be a marriage, not a divorce; then the
manifold isolations of the contemporary spirit, its wars and ill-
nesses, may truly and for the first time enjoy a chance to fade
away like old soldiers.

Despite all the drink last night—and I realize, flagging now at
a quarter to twelve, that gin followed by beer, followed by wine,
chased down ultimately by ample whisky, is an ambitious programme at the most youthful of times—despite all that drink, I
am curiously optimistic this morning. That I should place such
faith in education! It is a trap I have castigated H. G. Wells for
falling into. He thought education would bring a better world.

Now I am thinking it. But I have a grave reservation, to be
mentioned in its place.

An educational revolution could, in time, bring a better world.
The information explosion, coupled with the communication explosion that is surely coming, will change all our ideas—including
ideas about what education should mean. We have the privilege
of standing on Wells's shoulders and seeing clearly visions that
that great man only managed to glimpse. (He was the first to do
so, and so was thought very strange. Thank God, he was strange!)
What education was and meant in Wells's time is vividly por-
trayed in his *Experiment in Autobiography*, one of the key auto-
biographies of this century.

Wells saw education as an escape from the intellectual poverty
of his early environment, a way to greater freedom. Perhaps
those who are motivated as he was will always have the vision of
education as a green tree, something that grows all through life,
rather than as a stuffy form-room. Young Wells was terribly

earnest, though his earnestness was tempered by a saving sense of humour. Here is part of his description of life as a teacher at Midhurst Grammar School.

'In a novel of mine called *Love and Mr Lewisham* which is about just such a Grammar School teacher as I was, I have described how he pinned up on his wall a "Schema", planned to make the utmost use of his time and opportunities. I made that Schema, even to the pedantry of calling it that and not calling it plainly a scheme. Every moment in the day had its task. I was never to rest while I was awake. Such things—like my refusal to read novels or play games—are not evidence of an intense and concentrated mind; they are evidence of an acute sense of the need for concentration in a discursive and inattentive brain. I was not attacking the world by all this effort and self-control; I was making my desperate get-away from the shop and the street. I was bracing myself up tremendously. Harris and I would go for one-hour walks and I insisted on a pace of four miles an hour. During this pedestrianism we talked in gasping shouts.'

I was bracing myself tremendously. . . . English literary gentlemen hate all Wells stood for. Not only was he socialist, he dared to imagine the future might change (an insight that commended him to the young Orwell), and he braced himself tremendously. But there was more than one side to Wells. It happened that he braced other people tremendously. Women loved him, and retained their affection for him even when they ceased to go to bed with him. The fact was, he liked women; and apparently he smelt good; one lady said that he smelt of honey. He was a man of many interests. The next paragraph after the one above runs as follows.

'Mrs Walton my landlady who kept the sweetstuff shop, was a dear little energetic woman with a round friendly face, brown eyes and spectacles. I owe her incalculable things. I paid her twelve shillings a week and she fed me well. She liked cooking and she liked her food to be eaten. My meals at Midhurst are the first that I remember with pleasure. Her stews were marvellously honest and she was great at junket, custard and whortleberry and blackberry jam. Bless her memory.'

If any man created one whole aspect of the twentieth century, it was H. G. Wells. How curious that Cyril Connolly omits him entirely from his volume *The Modern Movement*, which aspires to discuss one hundred key books that have informed the contemporary spirit since 1880. You know very well whom you will find: Norman Douglas, Ford Madox Ford, E. M. Forster, John Betjeman, Louis MacNeice, good old Ernest Hemingway, and, save the mark, Ivy Compton Burnett. No H. G. Wells, creator of *The Time Machine*, *A Modern Utopia* and *The Island of Dr. Moreau*.

All of which may take us some way from education, but no distance from Chris's and my discussion, for we are both admirers of Wells. To him, we shall return here; and in homage, this volume of speculation shall be named—if I complete it!— after one of Wells's most characteristic titles.

Before leaving Wells, I want to quote again from his autobiography, to show what a liberating effect science had on him and his generation, born in the shadow of Darwin. Wells had seen the defeat of the Church in the great Evolution debate, and was contemptuous of it, saying that even the Roman Catholic controversialists discovered 'that the Church had always known all about Evolution and the place of man in Nature, just as it had always known about the place of the solar system in space'.

For Wells—and for his generation, and generations before and after—the Church had become the enemy. The Church, following the monastic preservation of knowledge, had enthroned itself as Queen of the Sciences in the Dark Ages, dictating on all questions, whether astronomical, mathematical, medical, or what, and was by last century one of the forces of repression. It was only deposed from its usurped position of eminence by Science (though Socialism also helped, to Wells's mind). I hope to suggest later that this position, still prevalent in my boyhood and today, may be due for more discomfiting developments.

In the 1880's, a new day was breaking, and the sun was science. This is part of Wells's description of his time in Huxley's biology class.

'Our chief discipline was a rigorous analysis of vertebrate structure, vertebrate embryology and the succession of vertebrate forms in time. We felt our particular task was the determination of the relationship of groups by the acutest possible criticism of structure. The available fossil evidence was not a tithe of what has been unearthed today; the embryological material also fell far short of contemporary resources; but we had the same excitement of continual discoveries, confirming or correcting our conclusions, widening our outlook and filling up new patches of the great jig-saw puzzle, that the biological student still experiences. The study of zoology in this phase was an acute, delicate, rigorous and sweepingly magnificent series of exercises. It was a grammar of form and a criticism of fact. That year I spent in Huxley's class was, beyond all question, the most educational year of my life. It left me under that urgency for coherence and consistency, that repugnance from haphazard assumptions and arbitrary statements, which is the essential distinction of the educated from the uneducated mind. . . .

'This biological course of Huxley's was purely and strictly scientific in its character. It kept no other end in view but the increase and the scrutiny and perfection of the knowledge within its scope. I never heard or thought of practical applications or business uses for what we were unfolding in that year's work, and yet the economic and hygienic benefits that have flowed from biological work in the past forty years have been immense. But these aspects were negligible by the standards of our study. For a year I went shabby and grew shabbier. I was under-fed and not very well housed, and it did not matter to me in the least because of the vision of life that was growing in my mind. I worked exhaustively and spent an even happier year than the one I had had at Midhurst. I was rather handicapped by the irregularity and unsoundness of my general education, but nevertheless I was one of the three who made up the first class in the examinations in zoology which tested our work.'

'The vision of life that was growing in my mind. . . .' Increasing knowledge of science has produced that elevating sensation in many of us. To keep that vision of life alive, we have to fight, just as Wells did.

3 Sleep, Dreams, and the Somnolent Computer

Friday, 10th January. I got very little writing done here yesterday. Luckily, I can write all today, while the mood is still on me, because I am taking this month off from my part-time duties at the *Oxford Mail*; Friday is usually one of the days I have to go into the office.

Yesterday, I was speaking to a group of students at the Institute of Technology in Oxford. Chris Evans is about to fly to America to deliver a series of lectures; he likes talking, finding that questions at the end of the lecture often throw up interesting points he might otherwise miss. Because I began to write originally from an inability to communicate, I feel rather differently about lecturing; but as one grows older and becomes less sensitive about what other people are thinking, many tasks become easier.

The group I spoke to yesterday was a class in Publishing, which is run by Peter Guy. He and his wife came to inspect Jasmine, our last home, when we were selling and moving to Heath House. We had lunch together before my talk, and discovered we had quite a few mutual friends in London, including Elwin Blacker, who is brother-in-law of two of Margaret's and my closest friends. This was particularly interesting since I still had running strongly in me the idea of the tide of associations which prompted me to launch myself into this book.

Rashly, in my enthusiasm, I outlined to Peter what I was doing. A writer is well advised to keep mum about whatever he is currently working on; don't let anyone know a thing, except maybe his wife, or else the bloom is apt to go off the plum, or the flower wither on the stem, or whatever horticultural image of doom occurs to you. Also, I believe, trumpeting abroad insensibly turns the mind towards the idea of *publicity* in general, and thus one's energies are deflected from the quarry. All of us, in these corrupt days, must hope, I suppose, to open our *Sunday Times* or *Observer* and discover to our horror a paragraph in one of those nasty 'Briefing' or 'Whisper' columns which begins, 'The extreme aplomb which has marked almost every paragraph of the work of eager young balding 23-year-old John Malpractice is still almost as much in evidence as his original shirtwear; only yesterday, he sat down to write a new and entirely unplanned novel, auto- biographical in intent . . .' etc.

Safe inside my original shirtwear, I talked to the publishing group yesterday for an hour, discussing one author's relations with his publisher. A curious question came up at the end. There was a girl in the front row with a lovely Plantagenet face (I heard her name was Elizabeth), who asked, 'What about Hutchinson's?'

The subterranean tide of associations was flowing again. I had not mentioned Hutchinson's until that point. Elizabeth then said, 'Aren't they going to publish a novel of yours?'

They are. In July, they are going to publish the first volume of a quartet of novels, entitled *The Hand-Reared Boy*, an outspoken novel which fourteen other publishers had rejected. How had Elizabeth heard of it already?

It turned out that she is a friend of Michael Dempsey's, the editor who supported *The Hand-Reared Boy* on my behalf. After the meeting, when she came up and spoke to me, I discovered she had actually read it. A great feeling of luxury! If you are a painter, when your canvas is complete, then your act of creation is com- plete, and anyone may look at it; if you are a writer, your act of creation remains in suspension until possibly a year later, when it appears in print and anyone may read it. So I count Elizabeth as my first genuine reader, beyond the circle of Margaret, Hilary, my agent, and the fifteen publishers.

My memory is a faulty thing. In less than forty-eight hours after the event, I forget much that was said round our dinner table. In a quarter of a century's time, when I first strap my ward on to my ancient and gnarled wrist, I shall hope to be able to buy storage-space in a computer for my personal memories, for future reference. It will be a way of keeping them fresh. Failing such aids, James Boswell's punctiliousness in taking notes directly con- versations were over still has much to commend it.

When Margaret and I take the children on holiday, Clive and

I always keep a diary of events. To date, records of our Swiss and our Spanish holidays are our masterpieces! Coincidentally, like this book, they have imbedded in them conflicting time-schemes. Part of the entry under Tuesday may read, 'We played Cheat after dinner and would be doing so now were this not Friday and we still three days behind with the writing-up. . . .'

One subject discussed round our dinner table was memory, its relationship to dreams, and the way in which it may have been modified by the development of the written word. Writing is a form of memory. Instead of rousing the oldest inhabitant out of his torpor to ask him what the village did last time the River X flooded sixty years ago, you now go to the written records; they have the added advantage that they may prove more reliable; or at least they provide a cross-check with the old gaffer.

Chris talked about that freakish kind of memorizing, the lightning calculator, who performs prodigious sums in his head. I had always believed that this gift manifested itself in illiterates, but this apparently is by no means the case. Perhaps I was thinking by analogies, for I recall from my book-selling years that the book-sellers who remembered best the points of a book were those who read least. I have seen these wonderful men pick up a dull tome, shall we say *Metoposcopy in the Ottoman Empire, 1453–1499*, and exclaim, 'Christ Church, I haven't seen a copy of this since the Wheeler-Hunt sale, when it went for five-ten! Pity it isn't the second edition of 1913, but still it should mark up at about—oh, let's make it fifteen pounds. No, fifteen guineas. Sounds better. Some American university will buy it.'

No hesitations, no forgetting. It was this sort of terrifying performance, as much as anything, which made me flee from book-selling.

If the poems of Homer were indeed declaimed by bards, then this is evidence that memories were stronger in the days before literacy. Whether telepathy might then also have been stronger was a supposition I brought forward, but Chris pointed out, as I mentioned, that because telepathy would be so much more direct and vivid than the cumbersome process of dismantling ideas into words and then having to rebuild them into ideas, words could never drive out telepathy; it would be vice versa. He

C   33

objected strongly to telepathy, although he had once believed in its possibility.

In the days when I was less fussy about what I put into my plots, I used telepathy once or twice. My objections to it are other than Chris's. I wish there were telepathy. It's the wishing I distrust. So much of science fiction proves, upon examination, to be wishful thinking, and thus an infantile idea. Telepathy is infantile. The only time I remember it being used at all amusingly in fiction was in Clifford Simak's *The Fisherman*. Alfie Bester used it with good effect in *The Demolished Man*. I once had a dream in which I remembered having been telepathic, and woke with a sense of loss.

When the brain goes off circuit, the memory is also uncoupled; which is why we fail to recall dreams. We sleep so that the brain can come off-circuit; it then de-programmes itself after its day's work, much like a computer; and that de-programming, if we happen to become aware of it, forms the scrambled mystery of dreams. So, baldly stated, runs the theory that Chris Evans and his colleague, Ted Newman, have elaborated. It is an attractive theory. At the same time, I observe how theories come in the dress of their day. Analogies between brains and computers have a special appeal to us; the analogy appears to make better sense of both. In an earlier day, in the days of the alchemists, alchemical analogies were used to further man's understanding.

Thus, on the subject of memory, sleeping and waking, Robert Burton in his *Anatomy of Melancholy* says, 'Memory lays up all the species which the senses have brought in, and records them as a good register, that they may be forthcoming when they are called for by phantasy and reason. His object is the same with phantasy, his seat and organ the back part of the brain.

'The affections of these senses are sleeping and waking, common to all sensible creatures. "Sleep is a rest or binding of the outward senses, and of the common sense, for the preservation of body and soul" (as Scaliger defines it); for when the common sense resteth, the outward senses rest also. The phantasy alone is free, and his commander reason: as appears by those imaginary dreams, which are of divers kinds, natural, divine, demoniacal, etc., which vary according to humours, diet, actions, objects, etc., of which Artemidorus, Cardanus, and Sambucus, with their several interpreters, have written great volumes. This ligation of senses proceeds an inhibition of spirits, the way being stopped by which should come; this stopping is caused of vapours arising out o stomach, filling the nerves, by which the spirits should be conveyed. When these vapours are spent, the passage is open, and the spirits perform their accustomed duties: so that waking is the action and motion of the senses, which the spirits dispersed over all parts cause.'

You may find much of that as mysterious, and perhaps as beautiful, as an alchemical instruction: 'There let the chariot with the wheels remain, until so many fumes rise up from the serpent that the whole flat surface becomes dry and by desiccation sandy and black. All that is the earth which is no earth, but a stone lacking all weight. . . .'

The aim of the alchemists was to become so enlightened that they would be at one with the universe; their obscurities were to keep their findings hidden from the wrong eyes. So their thought is not really so alien today. Not, at least, to followers of Jung.

Telepathy would, of course, make man one with man. If it took the similarity of vision without eyelids, then we should be bathed all in one thought-medium, like the fishes of the sea in the all-pervasive medium of thought. But if the power had lids and eyeballs, then we could direct it, to unify with the women we loved; to ease negotiation; to improve conversation; and in wise men we could read all the ramifications of their wisdom. But it seems as if only machines, as they tend towards more instant and complete communication, will achieve something like this ideal. From the realization of our ideas, we shall be firmly excluded.

Another way in which the Evans Theory is of its day (which is another way of saying that its newness has just descended a step from tomorrow) is that it combines hard and soft sciences.

After lunch, I want to examine some of the developments that lie behind it.

Lunch was simple. Margaret came back from Abingdon with sausage rolls, which we ate between soup (based on the last of the Evans' bourguignon) and cheese. Odd how Brie seems not to ripen as it used to; perhaps, as the demand increases, mass-production methods have been introduced which are not so successful as the old ways. I imagine shining antiseptic dairies replacing fruitfully unhygienic French caverns. Like Browne, I'm stuck between my ancient heritage and my future. The future excites my intellect; but the hulking half of me is stuck in a fruitfully unhygienic cavern! Nor do I produce the phrase by a Freudian slip. Man, until he evolves further, is so constructed that he can only advance fruitfully by keeping in touch with the ancestral side of himself— the heart keeping up with the head, as Toynbee puts it.

There lies one reason for the importance of the Evans-Newman Theory, for through dreams and an understanding of the workings of our minds, we are able at once to progress and remain in touch with ourselves.

Before we launch into that story, which forms another facet of our conversation a couple of nights ago, the history of dreaming is worth a brief glance; and then we can come to the Evans theory as Evans himself describes it.

The old authors Burton mentions, Artemidorus and the others, may seem now as amiably free with their interpretations as Browne's Female Friends. Such is not the case. The Roman Artemidorus, who lived in the second century A.D., was very active in collecting dreams, and travelled extensively on his quests. Other dream books compiled at the same time have not come down to us, but Artemidorus's *Oneirocritica* has survived, running through many printings and translations over the centuries, and has provided a basis for many subsequent dream books right down to the present day.

In the field of dreams, in fact, Artemidorus is the great name before the publication of Freud's *Interpretation of Dreams* in 1899. Artemidorus employed the principle of association in divining the meaning of dreams; this is also one of the central principles of Freud's method, the main difference in approach being that to the ancients the association lay in the mind of the interpreter, while to Freud the association lay in the mind of the dreamer. Artemidorus was a sophisticated interpreter; moreover, we owe to his work the fact that we can check on the persistence of dream symbols over almost two millennia. Despite the number of centuries between them, he stands as closely to Sigmund Freud as alchemy does to chemistry.

The notable thing about the history of dream-study from the earliest days is that theory preponderated greatly over fact, and speculation over observation. Fact only came into its own in the fifties of this century; we might even set a date as a milestone: a brief report by Professor Nathanial Kleitman, of the University of Chicago, in the journal *Science*, issue of 4th September 1953.

It often happens that by looking closely at something we see further. This process occurs in science; van Leeuwenhoek's discovery of the 'little animals' wriggling at the bottom of his single-lens microscope opened vistas of new worlds. The process occurs in literature;

> Shall I compare thee to a summer day?
> Thou art more lovely and more temperate:
> Rough winds do shake the darling buds of May,
> And summer's lease hath all too short a date

where Shakespeare's observation of a sixteenth-century hedge has recalled an early summer day to us ever since. To scientists as to poets, 'a local habitation and a name' are of vital importance.

Professor Kleitman and his assistant Eugene Aserinsky had observed something else that nobody else in the history of the world had made anything of: that the eyeballs of sleeping people move at certain periods during sleep.

Kleitman named these movements REMs, or Rapid Eye Movements. He believed that they coincided with periods of dreaming. There was a way to check on the truth of the theory—by awakening the sleeper and asking him if he was dreaming. He was. Always.

Research into the nature of sleep had been in progress before this. The development of electroencephalographs, or EEGs, had led—as one darned thing always leads to another—to the discovery that the brain sends out characteristic waves: an Alpha rhythm that signs itself on the graph paper of the EEG with a rippling wave of from 8 to 13 cycles per second, and a Delta rhythm that has a frequency of from $\frac{1}{2}$ to 2 cycles per second, a slow wave. Alpha is characteristically a waking wave, Delta a deep sleep wave.

Kleitman used these discoveries and monitored brain waves and other movements to build up a complex profile of sleep. It was when he began to monitor eye movements that he found how REMs persisted, in phases of activity that lasted from three to over fifty minutes. Subsequent tests have proved that REMs universally provide an objective indication of dreaming.

Later, with another research assistant, William Dement, whose name has since become famous in its own right, Kleitman was able to resolve mysteries that shrouded the nature of dreams since the beginning of time. Three discoveries are of particular importance (though Dement's study of the dreams of schizophrenics has great relevance to the Evans Theory, and will be described later); I give the three as listed by Edwin Diamond in his book, *The Science of Dreams.*

One. A fast brain-wave pattern of 10 cycles per second accompanied the periods of REM activity, thus providing an additional check on when dreaming occurred.

Two. This fast wave registered on the EEG four or five times in an average eight-hours' sleep.

Three. Each of these four or five periods of dream was longer than the one preceding; so that the final period might last four times longer than the first.

Later research has fully confirmed these findings. Almost every normal adult and child goes through the same performance (and in many ways 'performance' is the right word). Fifteen minutes after you have closed your eyes, the Alpha waves break up, reveries akin to dream crowd up, and the oblivion of deep sleep, signalled by Delta waves, rolls through. Like a tide, this deep sleep recedes, giving place to a lighter one; then the first period of dreaming begins, ninety minutes after you fall asleep, lasting for possibly nine minutes. When this dream period ends, sleep again becomes deep, though not quite as deep as before; it leads again to a second dream-period after a second ninety-minute interval. This second dream-period lasts for nineteen minutes. It is followed by another sleep trough, this time shallower again than its predecessor, and so on, with succeeding periods of dream lasting twenty-four and twenty-eight minutes. If you wake after seven hours, you will have experienced an hour and twenty minutes of dream.

The brain bursts through oceans of sleep like a whale, surfacing regularly.

Once one becomes used to this idea, it does not seem so very strange. When I first came on the details of this research and discussed it with people, I found that many of them rejected the evidence very strongly. It is clear that we all hold dreams to be our most personal property. People feel aggrieved that they all dream according to a common pattern. In an age when we fear bureaucracy and the increased regimentation and documentation that is one concomitant of mounting population, it is understandable that some cling tenaciously to the chaotic world of dreams. There at least, because C happens it does not follow that D follows. Like surrealist paintings, dreams don't observe cause and effect.

A graph of the operation looks like this:

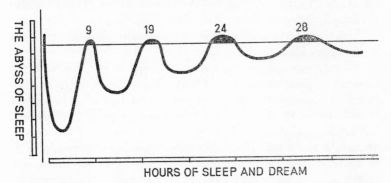

HOURS OF SLEEP AND DREAM

Some people deny strenuously that they dream. They never dream, they say. Or they dream rarely. *Their* nights are not peered out in fantastical visions.

But they are confessedly deceived. Every night, the cinema-in-the-round goes on, holding its showings at regular intervals. Those who say they don't dream, merely don't remember.

Highbrows dream no more than lowbrows; film directors no more dramatically than traffic wardens; nuns no more chastely than I.

As for the notion that dreams happen in a flash—that too has to go, although several people have tried to prove to me that *in their case* dreams are over in a flash.

Nor does cheese make us have nightmares, or a heavy stomach increase our dreaming (though it may disrupt our sleeping). However much popcorn you take along to the cinema-in-the-round, the house-lights dim and come up at the same set times, and for the same lengths of performance, though drugs can ruin the show.

Too many thousands of man-hours were dreamed away in the beds of Abbott Hall in the University of Chicago for the evidence to be gainsaid.

39

It boils down to this: dreaming is a regular and necessary function. The Evans-Newman Theory seeks to explain the function.

Experimental subjects deprived of sleep increase their dream periods, as if to make up for lost time. If the period of sleep-deprivation is extended to several days, then the illusions of sleep thrust themselves through into the waking hours, producing effects not unlike mild cases of delirium tremens. These are also explained under the Evans-Newman Theory.

With these facts in mind, it is worth recalling how Chris Evans outlined his ideas to the readers of *New Worlds* in 1967:

'Twenty years ago, if one wanted to get a dull answer to an interesting question one would buttonhole a psychologist and ask him if machines could be said to possess intelligence. His answer would almost certainly revolve around two counter-questions. "What do you mean by Intelligence?" and (worse) "What do you mean by a Machine?" If one then tried one's luck with an engineer, or some other type of scientist concerned with machines, one might, surprisingly, do a lot better, for engineers, who know quite a lot about the way the Universe ticks, tend to have less inhibited imaginations than psychologists, who, generally speaking, know practically nothing about anything.

'It was, in fact, the mathematician-cum-engineer, the great and eccentric Englishman Alan Turing, who first faced up squarely to the problems of machine intelligence in an extremely important paper published in *Mind* in 1950. This article, "Can a Machine Think?", had a profound effect on scientific and philosophical thought at the time, but the drawing of analogies between hyper-complex computing machinery and the beautifully miniaturized circuitry of the brain was generally frowned upon by psychologists and engineers alike. The blossoming science of Cybernetics did its best to close the gap though, and today we find ourselves exploring these analogies further and further, and finding them increasingly useful. In fact, quite recently, a striking analogy between complex computer and dream processes allows one to take an entirely fresh look at one of the most elusively mysterious aspects of life—sleep.

'Research into the nature of sleep—and its inevitable component, dreams—has been plodding along without really getting anywhere for a century. Three major views, or systems of belief, have dominated the scene. The first states that the most obvious reason for sleep is that it provides a necessary rest period for the body, and also for the brain. A "good night's sleep", therefore, should consist of eight hours or so of near-motionless body, and of solid, dreamless sleep. Alas, physicians have known for quite some time that sleep is not essential for bodily rest, and more recently, the electroencephalograph reveals that while the patterning of electrical activity in the brain *changes* with sleep, there doesn't appear to be any *less* going on. So that's one old stager put out to pasture. A much more ancient, but still shockingly widely-held view is that sleep is a "near-death" condition when the mind or spirit can leave the body; dreams are this entity's adventures during its sizeable period of freedom. The evidence for the existence of telepathic and premonitory dreams (aircraft crashing, uncles dying, etc.) seems to bolster this view, and J. W. Dunne's hair-raising book, *An Experiment with Time*, seems to imply that temporal as well as spatial boundaries collapse during sleep. But the evidence for telepathy and precognition, once impressive, now looks pretty thin, and leaving the question of religious belief aside most people will find this traditional view of sleeping and dreaming a bit out of touch with our present-day understanding of the world. The third classic approach, the psychoanalytic, has had, of course, a really tremendous effect on Western society, the keystone being Freud's magnificent insight as to the role of unconscious mental processes in our waking and sleeping life. Dreams, by this theory, represent the bursting to the surface, during sleep, of the huge fund of repressed emotions and desires which are part of Man's inevitable psychological being, and yet which Society demands he deny. The power of the psychoanalytic approach is obvious to anyone who has spent even a little time in considered analysis of his own dream content, but it has, from the start seemed a bit stretched to cover *all* the experiences of one's dream life. Dreams without great emotional tags, and frequently related to simple day-to-day happenings are common in everyone's experience, and it is difficult, despite the ingenious notion of a "disguise mechanism" to see these as reflecting suppressed dynamic forces.

'Having suggested that none of the three venerable theories of sleeping and dreaming can be considered to be comprehensive or really satisfactory, we find ourselves stuck with the amazing fact that we spend one third of our lives in a weird unconscious state, apparently merely vegetating, at the mercy of any silent attacker, and in danger of madness and death if we are deprived of this non-process for any length of time. (We can last far, far longer without food than we can without sleep.) We might not have been much the wiser even now were it not for a snappy observation by Eugene Aserinsky, a PhD. student at the University of Chicago.

'This young physiologist had been studying the curious movements of infants' eyes during sleep. Convinced that these had some significance, he drew the attention of the great sleep scientist, Dr. Nathanial Kleitman, to the phenomenon, and before long careful observations on adults revealed that on and off throughout the night, periods of rapid eye movements (REMs) took place behind closed lids. It was soon also found that people woken during these REM-periods reported dreams, while, if woken at other times, reported apparently dreamless sleep. Two knock-out facts had emerged; firstly, an objective, behavioural index of dreams seemed possible at last; secondly, the amount of time spent in dreaming turned out to be quite unpredictably large—as much as a quarter of a night's sleep in normal adults. A third fact coming from a brilliant experiment performed by Dr. William Dement of the Mount Sinai Hospital in New York, rammed the message home even harder. Dement found that individuals woken time after time during REM-sleep became mentally disturbed after a few nights, while a control group, woken for a similar amount of time, but during non-REM periods, showed no detectable mental upset. It looked as though the lid was off. The purpose of sleep was to enable us to dream!

'All this happened in 1960. A year later, as an impoverished PhD. student myself, with, apart from a number of beautiful girl friends, no visible means of support, I found my thoughts constantly, almost obsessionally drifting away from the subject of my thesis ("Some further studies of Pattern Perception using the technique of Retinal Stabilization") and churning over the staggering new material on sleep and dreams. It seemed obvious to me that the whole field had been turned topsy-turvy. Sleep was no longer a rest period, dreams no longer a mistake. But what then could the function of dreams be? My first ideas centred around what I thought of as a "mental defaecation"; all data absorbed during the day could hardly be stored (I believed), so perhaps it was held in some kind of short-term memory store until the night, when with sleep intervening to prevent further input, the day's memories could be scanned and the "waste" material rejected. Dreams, I reasoned—or what we normally talk of as dreams—take place when the mental defaecation or sorting process is interrupted by the sleeper waking. The material is then remembered, and the purpose of the dream forestalled. I was obsessed with the idea, but nevertheless realized that an important piece in the scheme was missing, and try as I would, I couldn't find it. Three years later, in the summer of 1964, over a very long lunch with a colleague, the distinguished computer engineer Ted Newman, the missing piece fell into place, and that same afternoon our joint paper, "Dreaming; analogy from computers" began to take shape.

'Computers, as few will need reminding, are very complex calculating machines, capable of a very wide range of tasks, and controlled by sets of programmes—instructions to the device to use its brain in a particular way. Now at the moment the range of tasks which computers perform, when compared with the range potential of the human brain, is small; nevertheless the programmes need constant revision, updating, de-bugging and re-classification if the computer is to continue to perform its tasks with speed and accuracy. The programme clearance process is performed first by taking the computer "off-line" (uncoupling it from the tasks it is controlling) and then running the old programmes through, revising them and finally checking them again. Were this process to take place with the system not off-line, weird tasks would be performed by the computer, and, of course, if the process is much delayed computers become muddled, grossly inaccurate and incapable of doing their job properly. Furthermore, as we move to bigger, smarter and more adaptable computers, this process will become progressively more important, and will take up more and more time. At the moment it is performed *for* the computer by a technician or programmer; before too long, some form of automatic programme clearance system, with a regular period set aside for the job will be vital if the computer is to work steadily, day in and day out.

'Remembering that the brain is itself a super-computer, brilliantly fast, with unparalleled storage facilities and speed of access, and yet undoubtedly controlled by some programme system, we can see that some process similar to that described above for man-made machines should be present. And this, in our view, is what sleeping and dreaming is all about. Sleep itself is the act of taking and keeping the brain-computer off-line, in order to allow the re-classification and de-bugging to take place without interaction with the outside world; dreams are the *actual running-through of the programmes*, a process which the individual is not normally aware of, unless for some reason he wakes (comes on-line) when the programme segment in operation is interrupted. If this happens an attempt is made by the conscious brain to "interpret" it as a kind of pseudo-event and a "dream" is remembered. The real core of dreams, of course, will be odd mixtures of stuff, almost all to do with recent events and experiences in the life of the dreamer, thoughts about recent or long-past events, current ideas and obsessions, worries, desires and wishes, and so on. In fact, anything done in the course of the day which requires assimilation into the great mass of existing programmes. The logic of the brain's programme system, of course, need not follow the lines that we feel it ought to. This is important to help in understanding why the dream-programmes, when interrupted, often seem pretty crazy. It's just as well, by the way, that our off-line mechanism is so potent and remorseless, for the experience of being fully conscious of a full-night's dreaming would be at best boring, at worst, unthinkably horrific. Anyone who has had a bad fever and suffered a period in which sleep is persistently disturbed, and the raw, hard stuff of dreams sampled intermittently throughout the night will understand what I mean.

'Once accepted, the computer analogy suggests some fabulous ideas. Some are a bit too fabulous to put into orthodox scientific publications as yet, but I can think of no better market at this stage than *New Worlds*. Idea one: many gross psychological disorders are due to a dysfunction of the *dreaming* process; confusion, loss of touch with reality, paranoid symptoms and persecution complexes are symptomatic of experimentally dream-deprived subjects, and also of schizophrenic states. Idea Two: if the latter is true, then a crash programme of research should be instituted by the pharmacological research organizations to develop a drug which allows the maximum amount of dreaming to take place during sleep. Such a drug might have dramatic therapeutic effects on chronic schizophrenics. Idea Three: barbiturate sedation might act by depressing the central nervous system so much that the dream process itself is inhibited, for at least part of the night. Thus, though apparently sleeping like logs, nightly barbiturate takers could be gradually driving themselves into a state equivalent to that of chronic sleep deprivation. Idea Four: the hallucinations characteristic of schizoid conditions and of advanced alcoholic addiction, might be waking dreams forced into action because of the dysfunction or suppression of normal dreaming at night. Grim warning for all experimental and joy-riding takers of hallucinogenic drugs, including LSD; the long-term effect might be to permanently interfere with the dream mechanism. Prediction: habitual users of LSD will sooner or later flip—for good. Idea Five: the more new material processed in the course of the day, the more programme revision and updating required. Therefore the younger one is, the more dreaming one will need. Old people who put down very little new material, and who have in general a very constant environment, will need substantially less dreaming and thus less sleep. Should they not be taught to accept without worry their natural tendency to sleeplessness, and learn to make use of the bonus hours they have gained? Idea Six: sleep learning is *out*. It might work, but only at the risk of muddling vital programme clearance activities. Not quite, but very nearly as dangerous as LSD. The reader might care to amuse himself by adding others to this by no means exhaustive list.

'Whether the computer analogy will stand up to the test of new experimental discoveries or not is uncertain. One thing is clear however; we are witnessing a revolution in scientific thinking which might well have considerable social consequences. Our understanding about the hidden third of our lives is growing daily, and this is but one of the ways in which the brain is being induced to give up its secrets. We already have computers which can read, understand speech, talk and write. Soon we shall have them learning, thinking and, as I've just pointed out, even dreaming. And what, people occasionally ask, appalled, will computers' dreams be like? It's hard to say, of course. I've a feeling, however, that they'll be no madder than ours.'

4 Baden-Powell and the Neanderthals

Sunday, 12th January. I love theorizing. Sometimes you wear a theory for a while and find it doesn't fit you; another theory may. I still recall that eloquent feeling of a majestic sunrise in my mind —visual, but also making a dawn music like Ravel's 'Daphnis and Chloe'—when all unaided I came upon Freud's theories in the library at school. How amazing! How forbidden! How unlikely! How convincing! New dimensions began to unfold—and, once the door was open, it could never be closed again.

A mass of new material on the mind's workings is now available. Some of it refutes Freud at some points, some of it supplements his ideas. Isn't it time we had an ambitious new synthesis of available knowledge, much like Sir Julian Huxley's new synthesis on evolution a few years ago?

I wonder if that synthesis would resolve a paradox I have never seen stated anywhere. Perhaps it is peculiar to me (nonsense statement, and I catch myself in it; we are each unique, but no one possesses one unique trait).

Anyhow, to my paradox. When I turn my attention inwards and examine the contents of my head, I cease to be conscious of myself as a personality; when I look outwards at nature, I frequently become vividly aware of myself.

This I observe especially abroad, when among strange scenery. Scenery moves me immensely: yet I become aware after a time of myself as an essential ingredient of the scene—even if as no · more than a tiny decorative figure in a vast Romantic canvas. The sense of self haunts mountains, valleys, jungles, and long vistas.

Then I look into my personal and secret thoughts. Egotism, ego itself, flees. I see only ancestors moving, deserted panoramas, and vast spans of prehistory.

I wrote nothing here yesterday. Other work claimed my attention. There were letters to answer, and I had a review to write. Even with this month away from the *Oxford Mail*, there's always too much to do.

Yesterday's *Times* published an obituary of Guy Wint. (I wonder who was *born* yesterday?) Guy was a remarkable man who enjoyed a remarkable career. He was well known as an expert on oriental affairs. After a severe stroke in 1960, he made a good recovery, writing a book on the subject, *The Third Killer*, in 1965. A line of Pope's keeps coming to me—'Farewell, too little and too lately known.' He was interested in most things and rather a mysterious person, and I only wish I had known him longer and better.

It's a disconcerting thing, moving into an age-group where one's friends die. Early last month, the writer Anna Kavan died. I admired her writing (her novel *Ice*, published in 1967, is perhaps her most remarkable work), and felt the same regret that I do with Guy, that I had not made stronger attempts to know her better. When I went to see her in the beautiful little house she designed for herself in Hillsleigh Road, I found myself having to fight that absurd reserve of mine which attacks me in the presence of strangers; but it did not stop us setting up *rapport*. If telepathy does not exist, I am an empathist of considerable power, able to divine through the viscera certain things about other people; of course, the divination only works over a small area of total personality, but an important area.

I've never understood how Isaac Asimov's androids could pass for human beings. They would be instantly detectable, however good their outward semblance. Indeed, I've often detected robots in our present-day society.

Although empathy must be regarded as a gift from the genes, it has its negative side. If one does not establish empathy with someone, one is apt to neglect to work on the relationship, and to fail to be interested. There are higher-flying systems than the visceral.

Dreaming is to a certain extent a way in which visceral and intellectual communicate in one body. We must take cognizance of dreams to be in touch with all our selves. Only that way can we be permitted to boast, with Whitman, that we contain multitudes. That the multitudes are largely of the past—the long past, in many cases—explains why they communicate to the intellect in symbols; in the beginning, there wasn't the word. The intellect, which is modern, must accept those blurred signals. In the proper spirit of acceptance, they enrich and fortify.

Western civilization encourages outward-looking-ness. In England, the military figure of Baden-Powell still lingers like a phantom in the minds of parents, telling their children to get out and kick a football or ride a motor-bike. Girls are taught to converse, boys to dance. Nobody is taught to meditate.

Communication is a fine thing—depending on what is communicated. Sections of the community, indeed, communicate as if their lives depended on it. Some writers I know, not content with stuffing the libraries with books, talk like automata. But the real communication lies within.

Our brains are, among other essential things, the repositories of human and pre-human geology, and for health we must send taproots down into the strata. We must communicate with the past we find there. The past is compulsively modern; the Niocene contains our experience of the twentieth century. My foot is scarcely beyond Proconsular tread, while behind every movement of my hand is an even older gesture, reinforced by millennia of usage by the repetitive genes. In this sense, it can be seen that we are the creatures of history—the future happened several million years ago, long before the Würm glaciation travelled along the region of the Rhine now called Neanderthal.

From external scenery, that future has all but vanished. In our heavily furnished interiors, it still haunts us, and ghosts from beyond the Hominidae appear at our family hearth. Until the spell is broken, all progress is a re-enactment. To break the spell, we have to understand our whole selves. We need to be more inward-looking, and quieter, to learn what we can from the freighted metamorphic rocks in our heads.

That introspection must be fuelled by facts. There are new facts about the brain. It is established, for instance, that the memory is no more an homogeneous whole than the brain. Certain drugs can destroy what may be regarded as the outer layer or short-term store of memory; as anyone who has smoked pot knows, holding a conversation while one is high is an odd experience, since one arrives at the end of one's sentences (if one does arrive) forgetting how they began, while remarks made earlier in the evening remain, by contrast, curiously vivid in perspective.

In the same way, there are forms of amnesia which destroy only parts of the memory. After a bad accident, say a car crash, amnesia reaches backwards to destroy the memory for some while before the crash.

Recent research indicates that memory is spread over the brain, rather than stored in any one pocket. The library is dispersed on bookshelves all round the house. One does not hear of any research into the creativity of memory, although it is apparent from daily experience that things don't store well there: they undergo metamorphosis as surely as carcasses compressed in rock.

Here are some examples. The miles of green childhood lane, revisited in adulthood, which turn out disappointingly to measure only a few dusty yards (and how long will they measure in senility?). The wonderful novel that knocked our adolescence silly with its majestic grasp of life, proved impenetrable a decade later by reason of its intolerable style. The fight we thought we won.... The film that had a marvellous sequence where they drive over the sand dunes to the ocean in fitful moonlight, reshown on TV some while later—and no such scene appears. You put that down to cutting, of course; but what about the people you meet who are two feet taller or two feet smaller than when you last met them? The side-turning you *knew* was on the left which has moved to the right in a matter of weeks? The paper-knife that you positively put in the bureau and certainly not in the bathroom cabinet, where it is later discovered? The friend who denies saying something you know very well he said? That well-liked portrait in the National Gallery which is gazing out of the other side of its frame the next time you go to see it? The super little restaurant you remember so clearly in a foreign town—and can never find again? As the song says, 'Ah, yes, I remember it well . . .'. But the custodian of the library has a disconcerting habit of scribbling in the margins of events.

Just as mental illness distorts our perceptions, so it must work on our memories as well—and it is as hard to imagine a 'mentally well' person as it is a 'normal' person (the greatest abnormality of all is to conform to an imagined norm). People spend a lot of time remembering. Our society is eaten with nostalgia. How much is this yet another fantasy operation in disguise?

We require a gathering together and a sifting of all the facts and theories on the dynamo in the skull. If, as I suspect, our culture is groping for some fresh path ahead, away from what has been labelled Heroic Materialism, then it might well find its impetus in a new understanding of man's function, as impelled by the brain. Then would come a period of re-education and that too would have to discard its present outmoded attitudes to the currents flowing in our cerebral vortex.

5 Science Fiction: From 'Modern Boy' to 'Little Boy'

Monday, 13th January. Much of my thinking life is spent speculating about dreams and the thousand other departures from what we choose to call the everyday world. Of my own past, for instance, which remains open to me from an early age—often irritatingly so. Of painters, who often capture moods that writers cannot. And of fantasy.

I discovered last Wednesday that Chris Evans shared some of the same grounding in literary fantasy that I did. We can distinguish many applications of the label 'fantasy', from the steepest fantastic flights of the imagination (under which such items as Tolkien's *Lord of the Rings* and much science fiction fall) to the fantasy represented by the stories of so-called realist writers; one could grade fantasy in its collective sense along a spectrum, with the Book of Revelations at one end and perhaps one of TV's deadliest realist serials, like 'Coronation Street', at the other. Beyond 'Coronation Street', one might place the TV news-reels.

It can be argued that the news is not fantasy, but this is true only in a limited sense. News reports confine themselves to events (generally 'unpleasant' events, since that kind has most appeal) which have happened. But we see the report, not the happening itself. Moreover, the report is conveyed to us by the same techniques that have just been tanking us up with 'The Troubleshooters', or some other item with high fantasy content. And many of the news items are instantly negotiable into the currency of dream; to the sophisticated viewer in particular, who sees through the realist façade of 'The Troubleshooters', and dislikes what he sees, the news items may be more acceptable as fantasy-fodder.

To take examples. There were suggestions that the showing of scenes of horror in the Vietnam War—people being tortured, shot, or burned—pandered to the latent violence of TV audiences. People always come forward and make such easy claims, whereas the link between cause and effect in violence is complex and imperfectly understood, just as it is imperfectly understood in the relatively similar question of pornography, as to whether it is safety valve or stimulant. (Pamela Hansford Johnson was criticized some months ago for assuming too crass a one-to-one relationship in the Moors murder case, where the killers were found to have copies of de Sade's and Adolf Hitler's works in their possession.) But even if we are not moved to do violence by violence, clearly we are mysteriously moved by violence, and the violence of the news, in this respect, is more potent to the sophisticated viewer than the violence of the thriller, simply because he knows it is 'real'—however much camera team, reporter, and film editor have had to do with doctoring the reality in one way or another. If there is a religion of violence, TV is its hot gospel.

For me as a viewer, 1968's nightmare event (and I use the adjective advisedly) was the invasion of Czechoslovakia by the Soviet Union and her jackals in the Warsaw Pact. On the rational level, one was appalled above all for the Czech people, as higher aspirations were crushed by lower ones. It was also a sorrowful thing to see dying the hope that relations between East and West Europe might continue to improve; it had seemed that some sort of liberalization was in progress in Russia; but as we watched the invasion on the Box, we could see that that idea was largely a Western fantasy, encouraged by the bravura performance of Khrushchev some while ago.

The urgency with which I turned to any source for news about what was happening in Prague made me suspect that the invasion affected me on more than the conscious level. And it was not hard to see what this effect was. Indeed, the Czechs themselves were suffering not only in the present but also in the past (which dwells almost undiminished in the memory); this they signified by scrawling Swastikas on the Russian tanks. So millions of people all over the world, and on the Continent particularly, were forced to participate again in that nightmare of the thirties and forties, when the map of Europe turned black.

Something has happened to people's mental horizons since 1945, perhaps because they have become more conscious of the divided nature of their minds. What was inside has become outside, and vice versa. The fantasy content of public events—the assassination of John F. Kennedy, the remarriage of his widow, the building of Brasilia, the rise of the Beatles, the invasion of Czechoslovakia—what you will!—is increasingly less latent and more apparent. For truth, in the old days, we used to turn to our fiction; but now we have to turn to the 'real world' for our fiction. The *gestalt* of the newspaper's front page blares aloud our secret life; and Dubcek burns like a star on our private wavelengths.

The Czech fantasy sent me back to the fantasies of my adolescence. The Wehrmacht were rolling back across Britain again, the S.S. clattering through barred streets, the Gestapo hammering on doors in the small hours. As a fifteen-year-old Billy Liar, I used to play a game with myself: whenever I travelled by bus, the ticket-collector was a Gestapo man. He was coming round not for tickets but identity cards. I knew mine would give me away. It was forged. I was hunted; there was no escape for me. Soon, the hand would be on my shoulder.

Or I was a Jew, and not wearing my compulsory yellow star. Sometimes they took me away without a struggle. Sometimes I made a break for it, jumping from the bus as it crossed Barnstaple bridge and diving spectacularly into the River Taw.

But they always got me in the end. Always, the searchlight picked out my running figure, the hidden machine-gun burst into life, bullets ripped over the face of the water, or the firing squad splattered me across the white-washed wall.

The Russian invasion of Czechoslovakia was a psychic onslaught against everyone. What games do small boys play in cities near that frontier, in Regensburg, in Linz, Vienna, and Passau?

Even news can be as much fantasy as fantasy itself. We are surrounded with fantasy. Or perhaps that should be expressed another way. We surround ourselves with fantasy.

It's not only the dreams that sleep brings us. Oh no! *Pace* Browne, our waking hours are rarely notable for their sober labours and rational inquiries! They are often as much peered out with fantastical objects as the night! The necessity for fantasy is paramount over our lives. And perhaps the dictionary admits as much when it gives as one of the definitions of fantasy, 'preoccupation with thoughts associated with unobtainable desires'. The old prehistoric life of man was full of unobtainable desires; but western civilization is powered by them. Maybe we have caged nature—but we are ourselves part of nature.

One particular variety of fantasy has always attracted me. Although I might have expected it, I was surprised to find it had exercised the same power over Chris Evans too. I refer to science fiction. We both meet many people with a strong speculative bent, many of whom read science fiction—or did in their formative years—but generally speaking the enjoyment of science fiction is not a popular pastime. Those who do read it often like to emphasize how unusual they are in so doing.

Science fiction is a particular form of fantasy; although, with regard to form and expression, it generally clings to a somewhat faded realism, in content it comes remarkably close to dream, combining as it does both ancient and modern myth-ingredients. In other words, it seems, typically, to be something that it pretends not to be: surrealism covered by surface realism. This is tacitly admitted in the never-ending argument over whether it is or is not 'escapism' (real-life-evading).

Such an argument can never be settled, and not only because fantasy simultaneously is and is not escapism: for to talk of 'science fiction' in this way is fallacious; as soon as one begins to talk of individual writers (I can name thirty science fiction writers in Britain alone), the problem disappears: for some are much more escapist than others, just as some are much less able than others. Many of them brew a mysterious concoction which is essentially

53

of our time, and worth examining more closely in its relation to fantasy and reality.

Both Chris Evans and I came on science fiction—SF I shall call it when wanting to indicate the hard stuff—when our years had scarcely attained the dignity of double figures.

What I intend to do here is to blend a summary of science fiction over the last three decades with the other themes that concern us, and so hope to show how it plays a central part in shaping the speeding zeitgeists of the years.

Before I launch into genial reminiscence of how young-Aldiss-in-short-trousers bought his first sordid copy of a sf magazine, however, it may be worthwhile to provide a more serious approach to the subject, and produce a literary-historical defence of the neglected medium.

When Sir Walter Scott published his novel *Waverley* in 1814, he sub-titled it *'Tis Sixty Years Since*, to indicate that its setting was that length of time ago. Scott's interests were antiquarian; but the idea of setting one's novel at least some decades earlier became popular with the earlier Victorian novelists. The casual reader of Victorian novels nowadays can easily miss this fact; what's past is past; but what has become a fine point now was originally a matter of some importance.

Mary Barton's *Wives and Daughters* and George Eliot's *Middlemarch* are each set safely forty years back in time. The same thing happens in *Barnaby Rudge*, in *Shirley*, *Cranford*, *Felix Holt*, *Jane Eyre*, *Villette*, and *The Mill on the Floss*, although the dating may not always be explicit in the text.

Thackeray's *Vanity Fair* takes place 'while the present century was in its teens': that is, it begins before Thackeray's own memory.

This policy of back-dating prevailed for a long time. Even as late as 1886, Thomas Hardy confidently opens *The Mayor of Casterbridge* with these words: 'One evening of late summer, before the present century had reached its thirtieth year. . . .'

It is surprising to find that Wells subscribed at least part-way to the convention when he was not writing about the future; the first page of *The Island of Doctor Moreau* makes it clear that the events happened a decade before.

A novel written today and set forty or even twenty-five years back would be an historical novel—or at least an historical novel in the limited sense of trying to capture the writer's recollections or opinions of a particular past period. (Anthony Powell's *Music of Time* novels admirably fill this niche.)

Time has moved on. Civilization continually gathers momentum. Novels are contemporary—or else they are set ahead of the present, like Golding's *Lord of the Flies*. This represents a natural evolution in literary technique, forced by the pressure of events. The convention is so strong that certain years ahead already seem to possess as much historical significance as, say, 1945, mainly because of the magic of numbers: 1984, 1999, 2000, 2001. . . .

These reflections occurred to me while reading Professor Kathleen Tillotson's brilliant study of *Novels of the Eighteen-Forties*, a literary critique going far beyond literature to examine writers' response to change—the dramatic changes that came with the railways.

Some of the reasons Mrs. Tillotson gives for writers preferring not to write of their own time are instructive: a wish to avoid the specific associations of strictly contemporary novels, whether problem or propaganda novels; a desire to escape from the moral constriction of the present; a wish to record change, either in process or by implied contrast. Any or all of these motives may be present in the mind of the science fiction writer also.

Mrs. Tillotson also mentions another motive: that the past, not being the present, is 'untouchable by the winds and waves that rock the present'. It is for opposite reasons one may choose the future: there, in the mists hovering about our tomorrows, is nothing but wind and wave. From the tempests of the future, the science fiction writer draws his main and most terrible tensions.

How regrettable that the capable writers of this century, the Hemingways, Betjemans, Lawrences and Compton Burnetts who delight the Connollys of the world, should cling to the past with its romantic and obsolescent exemplars, leaving so vital a medium as SF—the literary mode of today—wide-open to the fools, bores and second-raters who have moved in! Which leads me naturally, I fear, to my own entry into the field!

My discovery of SF was the archetypal one for my generation. In England in the thirties, branches of Woolworth's used to have a counter boldly labelled 'Yank Mags'. I ran up against my first counter of Yank Mags in the Gorleston-on-Sea Woolworth's in

1938. To a very large extent, my future was decided there and then.

The covers displayed a variety of delights bearing only marginal relationship to the contents.

Stirring Detective showed a man clinging with one hand to a buoy in a very rough sea while he strangled a half-naked girl with the other; his face, hardly surprisingly, was contorted, since two detectives in raincoats were firing revolvers at him from a launch just a wave or two away.

Pulsating Ranch Romances showed a horse with wild eyeballs lowering a man down a cliff-face to the rescue of a half-naked girl caught in a cactus, while two rustlers on horse-back fired six-guns at him from the canyon below.

Practical Handicrafts showed a man in a fedora smiling proudly at a big red fire truck he had built himself from instructions enclosed, while a half-naked girl looked on.

Weird Ghoul Stories showed a half-naked witch-girl forcing a man in a fedora backwards into a coffin, while two mummies tottered out of the shadows to lend her a hand.

Staggering Science Tales showed a man in blue uniform falling backwards from a crypt of some sort which was opening to emit an unearthly glare and a half-naked girl with a crystal on her forehead, while two robots moved menacingly towards him out of the shadows.

Diverse as these scenes were, an underlying pattern was discernible. Adults would have discerned it, and dismissed the whole lot as trash. For me, they were all trash, bar one. It was the Gripping Complete Novelette, *Menace of the Time Vault*, plus the rest of that issue of *Staggering Science Tales*, which I wanted to read. I paid my threepence and became an SF addict.

I knew immediately that I liked the stuff. I also knew I liked some stories more than others. And I perceived that most of it was clumsily and badly written, slightly marring my enjoyment.

It took only a short while, the time depending on how much pocket money I could wangle, to discover that Woolworth's dealt specifically in three main kinds of SF, the stuff contained in *Astounding*, the stuff contained in *Amazing*, and the stuff contained in the rest, a mixed bunch of magazines—some of which carried the best and most amazing stories I have ever read; fortunately, I have never been able to trace them since.

All these magazines were brought over in bales as ballast on ships plying the Atlantic route; I've spoken to newsagents who recall going down to the docks to buy them. In that way, SF spread to Britain, rather in the way the Germans shipped Lenin like a plague virus from Switzerland over to Russia in 1917, to complete the break-up of the old order.

Even in those distant years, when innocence had all but fled and puberty all but arrived, I was no novice to science fiction. In the year 1933, when I was eight, I gave up *The Gem* and took *The Modern Boy* instead. The emphasis in this weekly was, as the title suggests, on modernity and (for my preference) on the future. One of the contributing authors epitomized all that I loved about that splendid fruit of the Amalgamated Press: Murray Roberts.

I know nothing about Murray Roberts. Yet I owe him as big a debt as I do Aldous Huxley or Thomas Hardy, greater writers whose influence touched me later. For Murray Roberts was the inventor of Captain Justice.

Captain Justice was an adventurer of the highest order, a man often called upon by British and American governments when things got too difficult for them to handle. His base was Station A, significantly set in mid-Atlantic. At the top of a great mast on Station A was moored Justice's beautiful airship, the Flying Cloud, which could be turned invisible when the need arose. In the South Atlantic was another Justice base, Titanic Tower, 'a masterpiece of freak construction, over a mile high'. Titanic Tower had an aerodrome on it; as well as a small private air force, Justice owned sundry hydroplanes and tanks and flying wheels and a speedy submarine-yacht, the Silver Comet.

Justice was an imposing figure, always smartly attired in a white uniform complete with white naval cap. He wore a neat red beard that made him look oddly like the inferior Captain Kettle of an earlier generation, and held cigars clamped in his mouth at a rakish angle.

About Captain Justice was ranged a small but loyal company (no women, of course). First must be named the man who made the marvels possible, Professor Flaznagel, an irascible and resourceful old man who wore big horn-rimmed spectacles and a white straggling beard. There were also bald-headed Dr. O'Malley, very Irish; the dapper Len Connor; and red-haired, snub-nosed Midge, whose badinage with O'Malley provided light relief while the plot was thickening. There was also Bingley, pipe-smoking commander of the Flying Cloud.

Modern Boy serialized Murray Roberts's Justice adventures for years. His stories also appeared in *The Modern Boy Annual* and in *The Boys' Friend Library*, which Amalgamated published every month; the library comprised short novels, price fourpence each.

Justice ventured everywhere. In those days, a lot of 'tramp planets' used to wander through the solar system, reflecting Sir James Jeans's theory that the bodies of our system originated randomly by the accident of two suns venturing too close together. Flaznagel constructed spaceships which enabled Justice and Co. to reach these runaway planets. I don't recall that Justice ever ventured on Mars or Venus. The runaway planet Nuvius was once retreating rapidly out of the solar system, bearing Justice, Midge, and O'Connor away with it; so Flaznagel invented a triple-power magnetic ray to pull the planet back from Outer Space.

Justice's most thrilling and credible adventures, however, took place on Earth. Giant robots, chilling mesmeric rays, slave empires, enormous ants, and menaces from the sea bed were all overcome by him. In *The World in Darkness*, the story I recall most vividly, the Earth plunged into a cloud of impenetrable interstellar gas through which no light could shine.

Like all pulp writing, Roberts's stories have not managed to last past their own epoch except as curios—their characters are stereotypes which no longer convince; the endless 'Suffering catfish!' exclamations of Midge, the incredible spalpeeny Irishness of O'Malley, and the stock rakish jaw of Justice belong to the clichés of another day. At the time, it was all new to me. And there were gestures towards reality. That airship, the Flying Cloud, for instance—hard to see it as a symbol of the future after the Hindenberg disaster in May 1937; so in February 1938, Roberts was writing like this, when O'Malley orders Baker to get the Flying Cloud from her hangar:

'But he shook his head doubtfully as he ran, wondering why on earth O'Malley wanted the Flying Cloud when at least two speedier hydroplanes were ready for service. For, in these days, the airship was regarded as slightly obsolete.

'For some months now the great airship had been used simply

for heavy freight-carrying flights over long distances. But to Dr. O'Malley, she was still the only aircraft in the world.

'Towed by electric tractors and creaking hawsers, the sleek and beautiful giantess moved majestically out of her hangar. Obsolete or not, she had been kept up to her full pitch of efficiency, just like everything else on Justice Island.'

How exquisitely, how tenderly, pulp is that shaking of the head doubtfully while running; nobody would really do that. But when addressing ignorant audiences, everything has to be externalized for easy assimilation, just as one visualizes the readership's lips moving over the printed text. And the writing itself is admittedly automatic; but it suffers from few of the glaring and fearful diseases of style that rampaged through the threepenny Yank mags.

The mags did represent a natural progression from Captain Justice. Sometimes they had a hint of romance or sex in them which was an additional bonus. One of the first stories I came across was Henry Kuttner's *Time Trap*, a short novel that featured in what I have since identified as the November 1938 edition of *Marvel Stories*; it had an exotic cover by Frank Paul, and I treasured that magazine throughout the war years. It did as much as any one story to convert me to sf.

The standards were variable. Some stories were very poor. Once it had got rid of the 'Lensman' saga, which I could not attempt to follow, *Astounding* was the most reliable mag. I gradually fell into the habit of reading *Astounding*. The habit was hard to acquire; diligence was needed to hunt down every copy, particularly after the war broke out in 1939 and paper was rationed.

In the early forties, under its forceful editor, John W. Campbell Jnr., *Astounding* was building up the reputations of authors whose names now predominate over the field, although perhaps slightly less tenaciously than they did five years ago: Robert Heinlein, Isaac Asimov, Clifford Simak, Theodore Sturgeon, Eric Frank Russell, Alfred Bester, and the incredible A. E. van Vogt. Just a little later, a newer group of such names as Bertram Chandler, William Tenn, James Blish, Poul Anderson and Arthur C. Clarke was emerging.

It is always easy, because pleasant, for writers to forget how much they draw on the traditions of their predecessors. The favourable and fertile climate which sf writers now enjoy was forged, in part, by editors like John Campbell and writers like Isaac Asimov. If such writers seem less full of astonishment in these days, it is because their innovations have become part of a now standard pattern. Of course, each generation must rebel from the prison of accepted standards and received ideas. For all that, what was built was built.

Asimov wrote many stories about robots for Campbell's *Astounding*; they were later gathered together as *I, Robot*; and there were novels like *The Caves of Steel* and *The Naked Sun* (for my taste, Asimov's most satisfying novel) which continued the robot series. Asimov codified robotic behaviour with his Three Laws of Robotics. Thus he—with Campbell's approval—brought law and order to a scene of chaos for, before this, fictional robots had invariably gone berserk whenever they appeared: their function was to supply a story with menace, and nothing more.

The old pulp robots were just bits of violence. Asimov's robots were as functional as those faceless dummies that come and go in the metaphysical interiors of de Chirico's paintings (indeed, Asimov, with his nostalgic caves of steel and long perspectives, bears more than one resemblance to de Chirico). More. Asimov's robotic laws brought law into science fiction; he is an essential figure in the intellectualizing process of sf. History has now, in a way, overtaken him, since those early metal figures—Janus-faced in symbolizing at once warlike men-in-armour and reproduction-without-sex—have ceased to remain merely figments and have become the end-products of a rational process of automation scarcely visualizable by the general public when Asimov was first writing in *Astounding*.

For some of us, Campbell's express may now have gone off the rails. Back in the early forties, there was no more thrilling sound than the shrill of its whistle.

East Dereham, Norfolk, where I was born, was a small market town, still lingering on in some after-dream of its own, hardly aware that Queen Victoria was dead. In the narrow middle-class circle in which my family moved, science was almost as unheard of as art. It was highly uncharacteristic of me to turn to the scientific side as represented by *Modern Boy*. I tried to convert my father once, by showing him a copy of *Astounding* and persuading him to read one story I particularly admired. But he did not read it through and merely ridiculed it. Since he had failed to read it properly, his ridicule was inaccurate.

In *Astounding*, I found there were people who thought as I did. People, in particular, who believed that tomorrow was going to be different from today, who believed that space travel was a possibility, who believed that mankind might become unrecognizable, in times future as times past—yes, that in particular fascinated me, as writers held a distorting mirror up to the facts of evolution. As for space travel, I believed in that because people like Professor A. M. Low had explained it to me simply in the pages of a pre-war *Modern Boy Annual*. The best way was to launch your moon-rocket from a well. The rocket had to be built in several stages so that the used stages could be jettisoned, and the well should be in equatorial Africa, because in that way you gained the advantage of the greatest speed of Earth's rotation.

My pre-scientific interest in getting to the moon had dawned long before that. At the age of eight, I wrote and illustrated a story about a powerful machine constructed to transport people to the moon. I recall that it had a lot of wings and a lot of propellers.

Astounding was an obsession. Later, I found other addicts like me. Kingsley Amis and Bruce Montgomery used to chant the strange auctorial names to each other in incantation: 'L. Sprague de Camp, A. E. van Vogt, H. Beam Piper, L. Ron Hubbard. . . .' In the forties, *Astounding* was a cult, an act of faith, something to be torn up by schoolmasters and confiscated by prefects. The awful thing is that at that age one defies masters and prefects but nevertheless accepts their verdicts; inwardly, I also thought I should not be allowed to read such tripe.

Kingsley's novel, *That Uncertain Feeling*, commemorates the addict's anxious wait for the next issue of *Astounding*, on the twenty-first of each month. That was after the war by a few years, mind you. During the war, things were even worse. The magazine was published only once every two or three months then—and you knew that in the good old States it was still bursting out every month, good old John W. Campbell was still lashing the unbelievers, good old Hank Kuttner was still pouring forth his stories under diverse pseudonyms. In an ideal world, *Astounding* would have appeared every week.

The only benevolent effect of this shortage was that it forced one to turn elsewhere for one's ticket. It was then I dug H. G. Wells—whose drably bound works looked so eminently non-confiscatable—out of the school library. I liked his writing very much. That is to say, I enjoyed it less than *Astounding* but admired it more. He made you actually think about things, instead of having to accept them without arguing back, like the *Astounding* writers. He held minority opinions but preached to the unconverted, not the converts.

I read Wells's books of essays, I read the straight novels—not just the early ones like *Mr. Polly* and *Kipps*, but the more taxing ones like *The New Machiavelli* and *Tono-Bungay* (what a rotten title!). In those days, Wells was still alive and kicking. The noise of him penetrated even down to my level, the big volcanic noise of that small piping man. *Ann Veronica* I read. It was still considered 'dirty' at school in the early forties, just like *Jude the Obscure* and Cronin's *The Stars Look Down*. That was one great advantage of Wells over *Astounding*: he knew sex existed, which all the Simon-pure Asimovs and Heinleins demonstrably didn't; only Sturgeon acknowledged that sex existed, in the sf of those days. In the process of reading Freud and his popularizers, I felt that the heroes of *Astounding* falsified by admitting no worlds below the belt.

Wells cross-referenced easily with another living author, Aldous Huxley, the author of *Brave New World*. Huxley knew about the worlds below the belt. I read all of Huxley's novels, and also staggered muzzily through a lot of his mystical preachments; in one's teens, one puts up with any amount of punishment from a favourite author. For my present taste, *After Many a Summer* remains Huxley's best novel, with opening chapters that put Waugh's *The Loved One* and its successors to shame, and a marvellous cruel sf joke to finish it all off with.

One drawback in my unsophisticated reading of Huxley was that, dazzled by all his marvellous passages of admiration on Vermeer and Pergolesi, which appear regularly throughout the novels, I imagined he was also holding Lucy Tantamount and the dreadful Dr. Obispo and all the other lechers and snobs up for equal approval. No doubt my moral behaviour has suffered ever since from such lack of literary judgment.

The Wells that seems most masterly now is *The Island of Dr. Moreau*, which was published in 1896. Wells was neither the optimist nor the literary prole that his detractors have liked to claim. 'Dr. Moreau' is excellently dark. From its first appearance, it was misunderstood by reviewers, who failed to see how obliquely Wells was criticizing his own society, just as I failed to see the same quality in Huxley's novels (and just as reviewers have failed to see the same thing in my *Dark Light Years*).

'Dr. Moreau' is the story of a grotesque experiment, an attempt to create quasi-human beings, the Beast People, by grafting together surgically parts of various wild animals and training them forcibly to speak and behave like men. By using the harshest methods, Moreau enjoys some measure of success; but when he is killed in an accident, the moral and physical disintegration of the Beast People is rapid and terrible. The narrator is cast upon Moreau's island after a shipwreck and survives the horrors of the two régimes, the Moreau and the post-Moreau régime, each with its different kinds of pain. Wells expertly encourages our compassion as well as our loathing for the Beast People.

When he wrote the novel, he gathered part of his inspiration from vivisection, but it is as foolish to see the book as an indictment of vivisection as to believe *Ulysses* to be a guide-book to Dublin. Some see it as a ghastly parody of creation itself, with God doubling as Moreau. This is undoubtedly nearer the truth. A passage towards the end of the novel, when the narrator has returned home, lends force to this idea.

'They say that terror is a disease, and anyhow, I can witness that for several years now, a restless fear has dwelt in my mind, such a restless fear as a half-tamed lion-cub may feel. My trouble took the strangest form. I could not persuade myself that the men and women I met were not also another, still passably human, Beast People, animals half-wrought into the outward image of human souls; and that they would presently begin to revert, to show first this bestial mark and then that. But I have confided my case to a strangely able man, a man who had known Moreau, and seemed half to credit my story, a mental specialist—and he has helped me mightily.'

When any creative force like H. G. Wells comes along, the critics all set about finding where he drew his inspiration. Bookish men, they look to books, not life. 'Dr. Moreau', they say, derives something from Kipling's *Jungle Book* and more from Dean Swift. True, very probably true! But all sf owes much in its turn to Wells; and not only sf. Does not even the brief passage above suggest a source of one of this century's small masterpieces, George Orwell's *Animal Farm*? And isn't the source of 'Dr. Moreau' to be found in everyday reality rather than in books? The animal is embedded in us all, blood, bone and brain.

The Island of Dr. Moreau is Wells at his best; and Wells is a giant among science fiction authors: a fountain of ideas, a generator of striking images, a tolerable writer of prose. Yet, as the great English masters of the novel go, one is forced to admit that Wells occupies only a lowly place. His *Time Machine* is justly admired; it has many beauties; and, when it first appeared, its bending of evolutionary theory to dramatize the grim facts of England's 'two nations', the workers and the rich, must have seemed startling indeed, and helped to advance those social causes Wells espoused. The Morlocks and the Eloi stand as effective if melodramatic symbols of the corruption of society, during a period when society was becoming aware of its corruption and seeking remedies.

But what a more terrifying and effective—though in some respects no less melodramatic—novel had appeared thirty-five years before *The Time Machine*! A novel in which a corrupt society was anatomized through the lips of a young innocent, a Morlock raised to Eloi standards, but perpetually haunted by a dreaded Morlock of a convict, both unable to free themselves from their fatal though unacknowledged relationship. In that novel, money runs like tainted blood through all parts of the system—and we believe in money; whereas in *The Time Machine*, time-travel has to play the same circulatory role—and we do not believe in time-travel. So Coleridge's distinction between fancy and imagination obtains, and Dickens's powerfully conceived *Great Expectations* remains valid and vital today, whereas *The Time Machine* is simply a charming *fin de siècle* prose poem of undiminished novelty. And Wells as a novelist, judged by proper standards, has small creative vitality and validity, for all his gifts, for all that one loves him.

Free at last of school, I still continued to read *Astounding*. The war went on, Wernher von Braun's V2's began to descend on London, those horrible little proto-spaceships that made the war itself seem like a vision from science fiction. And then the A-bombs were dropped on Hiroshima and Nagasaki.

Those bombs were designed as weapons against Nazi Germany. Germany collapsed and they were used against Japan. Japan was then more or less in collapse herself; but the war had to be ended, preferably before Soviet Russia turned her forces against Japan. And so the last act of World War II was the first act of the Cold War.

I had had a hot war. The Second British Division, of which I was an insignificant member, was resting in India after its exertions in Burma when the news of Hiroshima was released.

Everyone was pleased. Nobody understood what the bomb entailed or how it functioned. And a good friend of mine, Ted Monks, a foreman-bricklayer from Yorkshire, came over to my tent to return a couple of *Astoundings* he had borrowed.

'You know what, Brian,' he said, 'this bloody bomb they've dropped on the Japs is the thing they've been talking about in your bloody science fiction.'

It was then realization came that the schoolmasters and parents had it all wrong. Sf wasn't just tripe. It connected. It was real. It was more than real: it was visionary.

Sf had been talking about the future and the future had arrived.

And this is where sf—at least the sf worth discussion—has its great merit. It is a straw in the wind blowing from tomorrow. It dares to speculate. Despite its many faults, it is a speculative literature.

Later, I shall qualify this. Nor do I pretend now that Chris Evans and I discussed much of this last Wednesday evening. It was received opinion between us. There was merely the pleasure of recognition that we had been covering the same ground at the same time. We had come through that same sort of fantasy, and seen it emerge much nearer reality.

With the dropping of 'Little Boy', as the Hiroshima bomb was affectionately christened, the world entered, however reluctantly, however unknowingly, upon the Nuclear Age and all its benefits and perils. Chris knew. I knew. Because of our peculiar persuasions in reading, we were immediately able to adopt new attitudes to meet the new age.

We no longer argue whether the Napoleonic Wars were a Good

Thing or a Bad Thing. They changed the map of Europe and the mental climate, and that change has been built into us, is part of our inheritance. In our lifetimes, we have heard a great deal of romantic argument about whether the Bomb was a Good Thing or a Bad Thing. Someone had to drop it, and perhaps it was as well it struck when it did, when the nerves of the world were geared to wartime suffering. The brutal birth of the Nuclear Age is already a part of our mental climate. We can leave it at that.

Now it is Monday evening. I have been writing so long today, so blessedly free from disturbance, that I had forgotten what day it was. It seemed like Sunday.

Timothy is asleep in his cot and it is supper time. Time for supper, and time to sit and chat to Margaret and gaze at the Box.

6 An Alligator in a Dog's Embrace

Wednesday, 15th January. It's a perplexing thing to be both anti-social and gregarious. I shut myself away in my study and am content to write; yet it will be pleasant to be back at the 'Mail' again. All yesterday was spent trying to catch up with my correspondence, and with interviewing a potential secretary. A likely one appeared this morning and I engaged her right away.

It is a week since Chris and Nancy were here; I have written perhaps a quarter of the book. The evening that I once held in the palm of my hand has virtually dissolved back into its component elements; there have been other evenings, other conversations.

The intention of the book remains, and behind it one of the intentions of life: that we have inherited so much, and hope to pass something on. These days, we suffer from a lack of confidence, the obverse side of our self-questioning; we forget that we are heirs to much that is worthwhile. Perhaps a new generation will find new directions. Till then, we do well to cherish our benefits—which entails having regard both to old ways and new.

The moon that was large and bright a week ago is now in its thin final phase. This morning at eight-thirty, before the sky was properly light, the moon had been netted by the bare elms at the front of the house, and I carried Timothy out in my arms to have a look at it. He pointed at it with his fist. 'Moon,' he said. On a similar occasion, perhaps ten years ago, I carried my other son, Clive, out to look at a full moon. I suppose he would have been about three. He stared hard at it and asked, 'Where does it switch off?'

Where indeed? He had invented a modern myth. In an age of animism, you see the moon as the home of spirits; in the TV age, you see it as something more or less under man's control, to be switched on or off as you will. People talk about 'the conquest of space', as if space too can be switched on or off at will.

By the time our forthcoming child, now twitching in Margaret's womb, can speak, he or she will look at the moon and say, 'I can't see any men on it.' Education is a process that begins at birth; the rudimentary concepts of mankind as a member of an interstellar community are already being built into the very beginnings of speech.

When we all have our wards strapped to our wrists, so that we are free of fact-memorization, education will concern itself with the important things. Thus hard and soft culture will combine; tomorrow's world will be multi-permeated by both halves of man's experience.

Of course, education consists of far more than fact-memorization, even within the narrower meaning of the word. Learning, discipline, cultivation, will still be necessary—will indeed be more than ever necessary. What I visualize is that the examination-passing side of education, together with all the old dates-figures-and-tables-memorization, rusty fossils of the Enlightenment which lies behind our examination system, will be swept aside to make room for an integrative rather than a semi-synthesizing experience.

It is this integrative experience—what I call here a 'fact-free education'—that will be new within the context of our culture; and so I shall talk about this side of tomorrow's educational programme, and not about the already established learning-discipline-cultivation aspect, which I visualize as flourishing side-by-side with the integrative fact-free education. What is already established is better equipped to survive; the new and tender need our attention, like children.

Education is currently in crisis. Students, blindly impelled, express their dissatisfaction with the current ways of learning all over the world, from the Argentine to East Pakistan and beyond. Even allowing for youthful perversity, it is obvious that the rising generation is not getting the sustenance it needs. This is the time for a purge, as it is the time for so much else besides.

One thing education will have to do is look at itself, and the educators educate themselves. Under population pressure, the universities multiply—while in life-enhancing subjects the curricula dwindle.

There is also a lot of what technicians would call 'noise' passed on in curricula—interference which has a distracting effect. Often such noise is hard to detect because we all share its attitudes, the attitudes of a hypocritical society. For instance, an extreme imposed unreality in the sphere of conduct, where idealistic or Christian precepts are mouthed in strange lip-service between mentor and disciple, neither of whom will live up to (or perhaps even attempt to live up to) the ideals they profess. Perhaps this is one of the matters that today's students object to. I certainly objected to it as a boy—all instinctively. My quartet of novels which begins with *The Hand-Reared Boy* displays the miseries and comedies of illusion suffered by one who followed, intellectually if not instinctively, such hypocritical precepts from parents and teachers.

Jung speaks of this sort of cant, saying 'Nobody ever questions the value of this kind of teaching'. Equally, nobody ever defines its destructive power. It blankets our true perceptions with layers of deceit; it renders us unable to transmit our private experience to others—and that alone, in English society, is one of its greatest impoverishments. We become walled off from each other by an early conspiracy of perfection: an imposed classical mechanics of righteousness that must be shed before education even begins to make sense.

Mainly because of this element of 'noise'—another feature of Victorianism still operative in our society—an important part of education occurs only outside the classroom.

Transcendentally better communication (i.e. ubiquitous, low-priced, three-dimensional, multi-channelled communication) may do away with the classroom itself; but classroom thinking, the rigid use of categorization, will also have to be banished. We have to be clear that 'Where does it switch off?' is not an ignorant but a highly sophisticated question. Asked in 1958, it says a lot about western man in the fifties; the complex machines were running, but there was some uncertainty about who or what was in control.

The same area of uncertainty exists about ourselves, and will continue to exist for many generations until education becomes fully educative. Educational noise teaches us to distrust ourselves —instead of the opposite. A complex machine is running inside us; how do you control it? So far, we have done little but fiddle with the vertical hold.

With the possible exception of the disparity between the Have and Have-Not nations, and the population abnormalities which bedevil that disparity, this problem of understanding our workings is of cardinal importance. Any work which promises a lead to the functions of the mind is most useful work.

That 'mind' is a concept, itself subject to the winds of theory over the centuries, is something we find hard to remember. Such words as 'subconscious', so freely bandied about, are only diagrams, and their actual relationship to any actual item as yet unestablished. Mind and matter are not as easily separable as they have been represented; Robert Sheckley, in his ingenious novel *Immortality Inc.*, where people in the future are able to swap minds about into different bodies, allows himself to be a prisoner of concepts of his own age.

But 'we know what we mean' by Mind. It is that within us which thinks, knows, feels, wills, dreams and directs. It is related closely to the brain, and the brain—although extremely inaccessible to observation—is real and physical enough. Man's brain weighs about fifty ounces, looks like a natural sponge, and is made up of grey and white matter. Not a particularly attractive sight. In many cases where patients suffer from mental troubles, the cause may be vitamin or hormone deficiency rather than a purely psychological malfunction; but where brain ends and mind begins, we do not know.

Since there is so much we do not know about the brain, room

for speculation is ample. On the one hand, there are those who regard the brain as the peak of creation, and the ultimate in complexity, a splendid machine compared with which our computers are affairs of rubber bands and tin whistles; on the other hand, there are those who regard the brain as something of a freak of nature—a freak, moreover, with inbuilt faults. Perhaps the truth lies somewhere in between, but it is worth examining both points of view.

The construction of the human brain is complex not only in physical structure but in temporal development. The consciousness dwelling in it lives in the equivalent of a glass-and-steel skyscraper, erected in a few record-breaking weeks; when we look inside the skyscraper, we find it has been built round a primitive little monastery, while the monastery itself is constructed on the uncouth stone remains of a druid's circle. To put it in more precise terms, the phylogenetically modern cortex or 'grey matter' is the outer layer of the brain; it enfolds the limbic system, which consists of a brain that has much in common with mammal brains, folded about a still earlier brain that has much in common with the primitive brains of reptiles.

These three evolutionary layers of the brain are labelled neopallium, paleopallium and archipallium. Professor Paul MacLean, who has developed a theory of the emotions based on a study of the brain, calls them neocortex, mesocortex and archicortex; these are the terms I use here, for they are the terms used by Arthur Koestler in his book *The Ghost in the Machine* (1967), a brilliant speculative essay which advances MacLean's theories, and a book on which I lean heavily.

The great French anthropologist and cartographer of the brain, Pierre Paul Broca, marked these three major divisions of the brain, stating that 'the limbic cortex is structurally primitive compared to the neocortex; it shows essentially the same degree of development and organization throughout the mammalian series'.

The human brain is thus seen to be a curious structure. Inside the essentially human, an alligator lies within the embrace of a dog. It is with this polygenous maze that we go ahead and challenge nature and the fates!

Our success as a species is entirely due to this brain and its mass-production (some 8,000 million copies of it will be in circulation by the year 2000). We do well to remember that the neocortex is a very recent development: not much more than half a million years old. Moreover, it has developed with amazing rapidity (there is nothing to indicate that its development is over). We remain close to our origins. And that statement has a meaning that bites when we know that we still carry those origins, or atrophied versions of them, about in our head.

Although this speedy development of the neocortex has (now literally) rocketed our species to success, it carries its penalties. For one thing, the neocortex and the limbic brain both retain certain areas of autonomy which sometimes come into conflict. Phylogenetic confusions arise; the phantom of a claw may always lurk in an outstretched hand. *The Island of Dr. Moreau* contains a layer of truth of which Wells's conscious mind was unaware. Natural processes employ economy of means; it would have been wasteful to create a new order from the old mammal order—a new order with a new brain; instead, *homo sapiens* stumbled into being with a 'tumorous overgrowth', as one anthropologist puts it, on an old brain.

It is this brain of ours that Koestler calls jerry-built. Pointing to a paranoid streak in human history, he claims that 'schizo-physiology' is built into the species; at times, and especially at times of crisis, the two halves of the brain, modern and archaic, pull different ways. Something was sacrificed by the so-speedy development of the neocortex; insufficient neural connections were established between the two phylogenetic epochs. As a result, there is inadequate hierarchic co-ordination between instinct and intelligence. From this weakness, mankind's historic troubles flow: wars, rapes, rivalries and violence.

In an astonishing passage, Koestler recommends a thoroughly modern solution to the problem, a way in which we could take evolution into our own hands. It is not for me to repeat his suggestion here; I have already over-simplified a complex line of reasoning; these things are better come on at the end of his polymath book.

The pessimism of this theory immediately suggests to me an amalgam of many bitter-sweet science fiction stories, where the central figure comes to or returns to Earth, only to find mankind long vanished and all his accomplishments dust; perhaps only a robot or an inscribed sheet of metal is left to mark his existence. Such stories, like Koestler's theory, help us to obtain a perspective on man; it is a considerably humbler perspective than the one suggested by the journalistic image of Man the Conqueror.

One interesting point worth noting in respect to the MacLean model of the mind is that while neocortex, mesocortex and archicortex are in no way to be regarded as physical equivalents of the psychoanalyst's Super-Ego, Ego and Id, or conscious, subconscious and unconscious, the parallel is something more than illusory, and Freud's inspired findings—so mad, so terrifying, so disgusting, to so many people—are backed up by neurosurgery. Infantile wishes may beset us; those wishes may come from a long long way back, beyond any human childhood. The Death Wish also holds an established place within the new theories; for the neocortex discovered Death, and the limbic brain rejected its discovery. So we have the perpetual conflict of man's history, between faith and reason, which Koestler calls 'one of the *leitmotivs* of history'.

That the brain of man performs the same function as the brain of any other living thing, namely, 'presiding over the physiological health of the organism', and that furthermore the human brain is in this respect rather less efficient, is the view expressed in a book by Charles Berg, *Madkind* (1962). Berg goes further than Koestler; his view of mankind is darker; we are neotenous apes and all for the high jump. But he too tries to come to terms with man's built-in split-mind, putting it this way: 'The object of these pages is to remind us that throughout the ages, as today, mankind has, one, been the victim of an intra-psychic phantasy life which has not necessarily any relationship to reality or truth, and two, that his behaviour, customs and religious beliefs and rituals have throughout been nothing more or less than the expressions, often in symbols, of this irrational, emotionally determined unconscious phantasy life with its conflicts and generally fantastic and imaginary struggles.'

From which it may be gathered that Dr. Berg's enormous book is impressive and exhilarating in the way that sermons of damnation are exhilarating.

So much for the school that sees the human brain as a sport with in-built faults. What of the opposite view?

If we are aware of the shortcomings of our brain, we should also be aware of its abilities which, to our definite present knowledge, are unique in the world.

First and foremost, it is this brain of ours that has brought us out of the jungles and savannas to triumph over all the other living things (except for mosquitoes, rats, flies, ants, and a dozen other phyla—but we may leave those out of our present calculations). Sorrowful though the more civilized among us may feel about the methods that were and are employed to keep us on top, it is preferable to be on top with a conscience than careless and trampled underfoot by enormous brutes—which was the situation with regard to our mammal predecessors before the neocortex went into production.

The complexity of the brain is generally conveyed by reference to giant switchboards working day and night and putting through millions of subscribers per minute, none of whom know for sure the number they want with any measure of accuracy; automatic dialling is used throughout; moreover, certain sectors of the system are self-repairing; the switchboards control all our thoughts and actions, right down to such automatic activities as breathing; and, what's more, the whole miracle is run on less current than it takes to light a sixty-watt bulb.

It is impressive, staggering even, the functioning of the brain! Yet comparatively few people have ever been impressed by it—the Bible, for instance, never mentions the brain (except once, in The Book of Judges, and then not judiciously, when a certain woman casts a piece of millstone at someone's head, to break his brains), though it goes on considerably about the heart, which we now know to be merely a pump.

Being impressed, however, can become monotonous, and it is well to hold a dual image of the brain: evolution's Ultimate Weapon (so far), and a reach-me-down makeshift with a slipping clutch (Koestler's model).

This dual image will have its bearing on the future (the future is the land of the dual image, of multiplication, of increased complexity). It is almost incredible the way that natural processes have produced such an elaborate mechanism as a brain out of protoplasm, and linked it to the outer world with senses of no more promising material: auditory circuits of bone and gristle, cameras of jelly! But, by the same token, brain and senses have gross shortcomings of which we are only just becoming aware.

Arthur Clarke, in his *Profiles of the Future*, has a word on this matter: 'The cells composing our brains are slow-acting, bulky and wasteful of energy—compared with the scarcely more than atom-sized computer elements that are theoretically possible. The mathematician, John von Neumann, once calculated that electron cells could be 10 billion times more efficient than protoplasmic ones; already they are a million times swifter in operation, and speed can often be traded for size. If we take these ideas to their ultimate conclusion, it appears that a computer equivalent in power to one human brain need be no bigger than a matchbox.'

We're back to the ward strapped on our wrists, for the wards will provide us with auxiliary brains more efficient than our own.

We are also back to dreaming. The more clear we are about the nature of the brain, the less likely we are to go astray in theorizing on the nature of dreams, and the more likely we are to have those bursts of insight which are still as much needed as funds to speed scientific research. Holding this dual-image of the brain in our minds, we can see that in dreams we are in touch, as at no other time, with a primitive layer of ourselves. To achieve truth, that primitive layer must be acknowledged.

Also, sketchily, we can see how our rational attitude to the primitive affects our character. Creative people, whether film directors, scientists, poets, or science fiction writers, are 'on speaking terms', as it were, with the old limbic brain. That part of the brain is rather like an old silent movie or, better, a TV set, always dimly burning, picking up interference from outside sources and creating its own interference; on its crude screen flicker dramas of feeling, smelling and tasting; this is its eternal soap opera. If telepathy originates anywhere, it is here. According to MacLean, the limbic brain's ratiocinative processes are mainly associative. Thus, its functions are non-verbal. It might be unable to visualize 'red' as a three-letter word, or as a specific wavelength on the electromagnetic spectrum; but it would associate the colour by symbols such as blood, fighting, meat, flowers, sunsets. . . . And we see at once that this is part of the creative method, the associative apparatus of any kind of poet. Only connect!

7 The Dreams of Twickenham (and Wandsworth)

Thursday, 16th January. I've been cheating. It is now noon, and the last few paragraphs were written today. I didn't mark the day for fear of interrupting my argument.

The argument flows on; it is clear in my head. But I've had enough for the time being. Linear thinking is not my strong point; my advance is circular—I console myself by believing that this, on a higher level, was the way Jung reasoned. The central point may even be less important, to certain minds, than the paths that lead to it; there's nothing you can *do* at the top of Everest (except pander to the limbic brain and plant crucifixes and flags there)— the climb's the thing.

So I stand by the window and gaze out at our garden and field, where Tony Luke's horses graze. The two foals, King and Queenie, canter round after each other, kicking their heels up. The older horses stand looking east or west, so that the sun can warm them with greatest effect. Perhaps they are all hoping for spring. Bulbs are appearing everywhere. Since we have yet to spend a spring at Heath House, we don't know where they will pop up, and can be surprised by them.

I resolve not to write here of how the County Planning Committee in Reading plans to turn our field into a car park, shopping area and Community Centre, against the expressed wishes of the village. That is a different sector of the battlefield.

This book has taken most of my attention over the last week; I have worked long hours at it. Tomorrow, I am going up to London, to see Hilary Rubinstein, my agent, and other people. I shall also see Chris Evans, and hope to go over to the National Physical Laboratory with him. On Monday, he is off to the States, so we are just managing to fit the visit in in time.

The Dreams of Twickenham (and Wandsworth)

Monday, 20th January. The world's first chronosopher, J. T. Fraser, and I were talking last year about the different flow-rates of time, and were suggesting that one of the big watch companies should take a cue from Salvador Dali and invent a soft watch that would register subjective time. We have hard watches that register Objective Common Time, and part at least of civilization has been directed towards organizing our activities more and more by the metronomes of Objective Common Time; but our feelings are synchronized to subjective time.

Our feelings would receive due acknowledgement as sense-events of as much importance as our actions if they were marked by some external record, in the way that hard watches and clocks mark the actions that belong in the external world. We cut a trail of wounds and roses as we go, but the armourers and gardeners are inside us.

This book is designed to register many time-flows; and to its structure each reader adds his own metronome. When and where are *you*?

The dated paragraph above carries effortlessly over four days.

I had a good day with the Evanses on Saturday. In the afternoon, they drove me back from their home in Twickenham to Richmond station, and I caught a Southern Railway train to Waterloo, where I could get a taxi to Paddington.

Wandsworth, Clapham, Vauxhall, Lambeth—those were some of the stations on the route. Poor eroded parts of London, encrustations round the heart. Walking through Richmond and Twickenham, I had thought how the subtopian effect there was pleasant, at least on a fine day, with everything on a humdrum but completely human scale—'handy for shopping'. Fine. And the twentieth-century graftings on to what is essentially a Victorian environment are not too badly done: because, in the main, nobody's interests have come too violently into conflict.

On the train journey, though, the results of violent conflict are apparent.

Once through Richmond and Kew and—is it Turnham Green? —the horror starts. Wandsworth lies under its own blight, its windows and tiles and roads and hedges a special Wandsworth brown nearest black. Clapham is built for junctions, not people. Here, one finds none of the loose community of interest visible in

Richmond. In the Wandsworth area there are only the exploiters and the exploited.

Not that new things aren't being done. The train halts, and one peers down in horror at acres of desolation where ground plans of hypogeal chambers are being formed in concrete: archaeological excavations pointing the wrong way in time. New roads are being blasted through uplands of crippled brick. Something that will one day become a roaring flyover aligns its massive Y-bones straight at the train, dominating it with giant catapults. No compromise is possible between the exploiters and the exploited. In the same way, no compromise is possible between last century and this. Each must stick to its own ugliness.

Wandsworth is closing its public library—the only public library to close down this century!

The Wandsworth school by the railway line was built in 1897, the year *The War of the Worlds* was appearing in serial form. Beyond the school lie Edwardian slums, and then a modern school complex, blank-faced and utilitarian.

The train pauses; the waiting diesel sends oddly human noises along its train: a bounding heartbeat plus the long shuddering breaths of a patient undergoing a critical operation. We move on, and now the old dingy houses are unbroken in their ranks. Only distantly does one see gaunt new blocks, moving slowly in like glaciers. Past Vauxhall, one catches a glimpse of the Houses of Parliament, from which the whole system is ostensibly governed.

Parents with two small girls were travelling in my carriage. This was as unfamiliar territory to the girls as to me. One said, looking down the embankment at rows of bleary terraces, 'I don't much like those houses. I don't much like them because they've got nasty windows.'

I kept wondering to what extent it was reasonable to look on the whole place as some sort of analogue of human life. Wandsworth didn't get like that by accident. Something if not someone made it that way.

And in all those houses, a third of everybody's day is spent peered out in fantastical visions. Good for them! Perhaps for many it is the best third!

Chris Evans showed me over the National Physical Lab. One feature of its layout, which in general much resembles Pinewood

Film Studios, is extremely English and would amuse my American friend, Harry Harrison. An ancient right-of-way ('Used ever since Neanderthal Man,' says Evans, laughing) crosses the grounds. It has been preserved, is heavily wired off, and bisects the entire laboratory area. When the inner gates are closed, as they were when we left, we had to use a footbridge to get from one side of the right-of-way to the other. One of the labs is built on stilts so as to span this ancient track without closing it.

Myself, I like to see modern scientific efficiency yielding to amenity. A pity it doesn't always do so!

So far, I have spoken only of Evans's work with regard to dreams. He has adopted other lines of approach in his central attempt to study the brain. I was able to test two of these experiments for myself.

Both experiments concern stabilized images beamed in to the two portions of the brain most readily accessible, the eye and the ear, and tell us something about the way the brain observes the outside world. Chris Evans's two papers concerning the experiments form Appendices II and III.

The auditory stabilized images interested me from the first. I wrote a pair of poems based on the experiment, the words in which have undergone repetitive deformation.

Auditory Stabilized Images: I
Sensory Deprivation.

In the gargle the snool eyes
Cousined by wall and heads
Deep under wither's stay
Bilising hang hang hang

Bears the tail empties the plague
Of my grieg detensials
Swords in numb dispense
While I sickles deep deep deep

Repeat 200 times

Auditory Stabilized Images: II
Conference Tables.

The Dreams of Twickenham (and Wandsworth)

> Outsize wee porters
> Gluts my co-fanes
> Drying to ram at eyes
> Mine are E-shoes
> Insight poly T-shoes
> Play their grey gay
> Trying to grow sober
> Magi rissoles
>
> Repeat 100 times.

The 'destablished' versions form Appendix IV.

One note continually repeated forms a tune. A slowly dripping tap creates its own melody in a listening ear. This would fall under the same law of deprivation of signal as an auditory stabilized image. It is almost as if part of the brain fought to avoid monotony. May the dreams burn bright in Wandsworth every night!

When Chris, his secretary, and I went back to his home for lunch, we took with us the first-fruits of another experiment Evans conducted last month through *TV Times*: two large cardboard boxes brimming over with people's dreams!

Early in December last year, Evans launched a National Dream Week, and the *TV Times* carried his Week's Dream Diary, which readers were invited to fill in each day; they could append separate notes if they wished.

Some of the dreams were beautiful, some macabre, many very funny—funny, that is, to the waking mind, which insists on linkages unknown to the levels below. 'We were all eating a huge meal, in which every course consisted of baked beans, when my husband came in and demanded a divorce; so I drove off on a motor-bike and ended up in a wood where some horses were galloping about among the trees.'

Every item in this dream is banal in itself. As with a poem or novel, it is the juxtapositions that matter. One doesn't have to be particularly sophisticated to interpret a longing for freedom, both from the confines of materialist day-to-day living and from a dominating marriage. Wandsworth at night must be full of phantom horses, galloping among phantom trees.

There is no doubt that these Arabian Nights sustain us. This they can do whether we 'understand' them or not, since they are 'understood' by one level or another; the idea that a dream un-interpreted is like a letter unread is not so.

In my childhood, I had two dreams that meant a great deal to me: so much, that I still recall them clearly.

One of the dreams occurred only once: I cannot be sure that the other did not occur several times. In the first one, I was walking along the cliffs at Bacton, Norfolk, with a cousin. Before the days of North Sea Gas, in the thirties, Bacton was absolutely deserted most of the year. The 'cliffs' were in fact little more than sand dunes on which coarse grass grew, and so I saw them in my dreams. My cousin and I were walking among the sharp grass, looking down at the beach and the sea. On the beach a tiger prowled, lithe of limb. It was large and beautiful. It was looking up at me, and its tail swished. I was conscious of how easy it would be to slip and roll down the dunes into the tiger's mouth; and this reflection brought me as much pleasure as it did apprehension.

The dream impressed me as being very important. Only much later did I see its meaning, which of course did turn out to be important—which was why I had 'saved' it amid thousands of discarded dreams.

Because my parents never managed to come to terms with their own anger, they could not come to terms with mine. I was made as a child to repress my anger. Any small tantrums called down sharp reprisals—not always physical (shakings and so on) but more terrible intangible things, such as threats to withdraw love. As a result, I grew up unable to face my anger honestly. That I have now come to terms with it is due in part to my wife but also to that early dream, which painted my difficulties for me; the tiger was my anger, and I was afraid to meet it.

I presume that when I dreamed, my knowledge of tigers was primitive enough for me to have been unable to decide whether the tail-swishing was an indication that the tiger would greet me affectionately or tear me to pieces. It took me many years to realize that the tiger, instead of devouring me as it easily could have done, was merely waiting for my approach (and to realize even that I might be happier on the beach than on the cliff, with sharp grass cutting my legs!); throughout those years, the dream must have offered a latent reassurance. In the end, I had a big welcome from the big pussy.

The Dreams of Twickenham (and Wandsworth)

I think of that dream nowadays when I come across a reproduction of Dali's painting, 'One Second Before Awakening from a Dream Caused by the Flight of a Bee Around a Pomegranate'.

It is impossible to keep art out of life—philistines are merely people who die trying. That soft and terrible footfall behind you and all about you is the approach of art. To match earth, air, fire and water, there are four other elements: nature, art, science and time. Each one is perpetually overhauling the other. It was apposite that my tiger should appear to a dweller under Leo, just as the mating of opposites is a principle of life. In their origins, art and science were interfused, inseparable; good science fiction writers seek to make them whole again—in Philip K. Dick's best writing, they are whole again; he is the great surrealist. But we are all our own surrealists in our dreams.

One of Dick's characters says, 'Everything is true, everything anyone has ever thought.' At the least, this is a life-giving lie; at the least, it gives us the freedom—needed in this century as much as ever—to go between sleep and waking without being a stranger to ourselves in either state. These days, I always awaken with the sense that something beautiful has been going on, though I'm not sure what.

Now I think about it for the first time, there may be another reason for supposing something beautiful is going on; for the beauty may be freedom and I always wake to a trap. It may be that trap of which I have spoken, the hypocritical conspiracy of perfection that seeks to lock each of us within the cages of our own experience. Much of my life and my writing is now devoted to attacking that cage and what forms it. The vision of the ideal is all very well, but it can imprison us, so that we remain, however many times we seem to ourselves to burst refreshed from sleep, imprisoned for ever 'one second before awakening from a dream caused by the flight of a bee around a pomegranate'. It can get so that we are even afraid to reveal our dreams!

That hypocritical conspiracy of perfection is now nearly worn through—yet it still has power! Who among thinking people now doubts that we in western civilization are under some kind of imprisoning spell? I've been telling myself inwardly that I'd stick to safe things in this book, alternate between seriousness and bathos as I fear I have been, never even dare to get on to the vexed

F
81

topic of that growing gap between the developed and undeveloped world which is of such magnitude that even the ignorant like myself must be drawn to discuss it; yet at present there is really only the one subject, isn't there?, the Whither of western civilization: and so I'll have to come to it. Last!

Before those uplands, the continued plod through the soggy meadows of my mind. . . .

My second dream is less of a textbook case than the tiger dream, in that it does not really require 'understanding'. It was just a symbol of comfort, couched in somewhat banal terms.

I was walking along a country lane towards sunset, perhaps wondering where I was going. Although the impression was that the landscape was flat, the road was so enclosed between high hedges that I could see little beyond. Two old people, a man and a woman, appeared and invited me to their home.

It proved to be rather picturesque. An old parish church, of what I would now judge to be the Decorated Period, with a square tower, loomed in splendid ruin nearby; only the tower, the wall it supported, and a long adjoining wall, were still standing. The stained glass windows in this long wall remained intact. The original tiled floor of the church was also preserved. In the corner of this ruin, a small Tudor cottage had been built, fitting snugly against the stone of the church. Years later, entering the shell of Framlingham Castle, where a Tudor house stands, I found my dream returning.

The old couple lived in this cottage. They invited me in. We paused to look back at the sunset before entering. The sun was low and red, filling the sky with colours that added their fire to the sombrely beautiful panes of the church. I was moved and delighted.

We were inside. All was quaint and charming. Over an old-fashioned fireplace, a black kettle sang. In front of the fire, a cat sat purring. With poverty went comfort and homeliness. The old couple, full of kindness, and wearing voluminous Victorian clothes, motioned to me to make myself welcome.

Perhaps most of the décor of this dream came off a Christmas card; the interior was certainly commonplace enough. Yet the effect on me was one of exaltation, a calm and mannerly exaltation.

Nowhere have I seen it mentioned, but it may be possible that some dreams emerge so clearly from some basic pattern of the personality that they are worth preserving, having relevance beyond analysis for long periods of one's life. Certainly, this dream, for all its seeming banality, has often been valuable to me. I was working to preserve it long before an intention to do so consciously emerged.

Indeed, I now recall that I must have dreamed it before I was six, for at the age of six I was sent away to live with my grandmother, and I recollect (now!) that I endeavoured to draw the church, house, sunset and people for her. I painted it several times throughout my boyhood and preserved one painting for a number of years.

When Clive was a small boy of perhaps six, and Wendy little more than a toddler, we were in grave disaster, and I sketched and painted my dream for them, in the somewhat superstitious hope that it might give them comfort. Indeed it may have done, for Clive referred to it only a year ago.

At most stages of my life, this dream has seemed oddly appropriate. Recently, I have seen it as a happy adjustment to the half-broken-down half-glorious state in which everyone over first youth lives. And no doubt, when I am old and feeble and less of an atheist than now, my return into the arms of the church will occasion me no surprise—merely a renewed acquaintance with my enriching dream!

Something of this I touched on to Chris Evans last Saturday, when we were talking of dreams. Just as the dream of Jacob, one of the fifteen dreams of the Old Testament, may be an important landmark in the development of the human psyche, so certain dreams may be important to an individual in the development of his own psyche. If such dreams, by the Evans-Newman Theory, were going into discard, then why did we intercept them? And, following from that question, how much of our daily intake of impressions is discarded? He answered something like this:

'Of course we know that very little of any day's impressions does actually get thrown out entirely. On a psychiatrist's couch, or under hypnosis, almost everything can be recalled from a long way back. I'm beginning to modify my early thoughts, and see the whole business much more as a process of sorting, of shuffling and filing.'

So the matter, I see, as I ought always to have seen, is still not entirely worked out. It may indeed take many decades, as many centuries have already gone by, before dreaming and the brain behind it are understood. All one can hope to do is set a few bricks in place, and hope they are key bricks.

8 The Imaginary Life and Death of Telepathy

Given the nudge, I begin for the first time to think constructively about the dream situation. I return to my original image for the brain: remains of a temple below an old church inside a skyscraper. Inaccurate imagery. The three sections of the brain are organic, and enjoy some margins of autonomy; perhaps dreams are somewhat in the nature of inter-office memos. Their curious nature—that is, the way in which they often seem to contain both apparent and latent meaning—is explicable as the effect of their being the only workable common language between the neocortex (word-making department) and limbic brain (picture- or emotion-making department). Computer-language is now tending more and more towards English (or German or Japanese); but it still remains at present a compromise between the natural language of man and the natural language of a binary computer; the human brain may have forged its own natural language in order to achieve inter-communication between all its parts.

Which presupposes that human dreams are much more complex than the dreams of animals. That is impossible to test at present; but we can presume it to be so.

A few days and pages ago, I mentioned that the quality as well as the quantity of dreams was important. The dreams of schizophrenics are very poor in quality. A good deal of research has gone into thought-processes of schizophrenics; we know that their thought-processes are often highly abstract. Feelings may become attenuated, until depersonalization sets in. It is not surprising that schizophrenic dreams show the same qualities.

In one of my stories, *Man on Bridge*, set in Middle-Europe, Adam X is a man-made schizophrenic; parts of his brain have been excised by surgery by Morgern Grabowicz, aided by Jon Winther. Adam X has a typical schizophrenic dream, 'of five minutes' duration'. He dreamed of a bench. Grabowicz says:

'Ah, that's interesting! You see, Jon? And what was this bench like?'

Adam says: 'It had a steel support at each end. It was perfectly smooth and unmarked. I think it stood on a polished floor.'

'And what happened?'

'I dreamed of it for five minutes.'

Winther says: 'Didn't you sit down on the bench?'

Adam: 'I was not present in my dream.'

Winther: 'What happened?'

Adam: 'Nothing happened. There was just the bench.'

Grabowicz: 'You see, Jon! Even his dreams are chemically clean! We have eradicated all the old muddle of the hypothalamus and the visceral areas of the brain. You have here your first purely cerebral man.'

And a poor triumph it turned out. Partial capacity is no solution in situations needing total capacity: which is one reason why the sick require to be healed, even from psychosomatic distempers.

One researcher in this field, K. Goldstein, suggests that the fault in schizophrenia lies in the isolation of parts of the nervous system from one another. This would cut down the number and complexity of inter-office memos, particularly if the mechanics who serviced the typewriters and phones were cut off.

According to Evans, the dream process is so vital that any interference with its function will lead to eventual ill-health. This is certainly a reversal of the old idea that ill-health, particularly mental ill-health, will eventually show up in dreams.

I hover on the brink of suggesting that the vast output of fantasy with which we surround ourselves, to which reference was made earlier, is the community's attempt to bolster its dreams, to enrich them, and so to enrich health—the psychic health so damaged by our isolation in cages. Such forms of fantasy as plays, films, stories and even news programmes (for reasons outlined earlier) may act like dreams, even when given massive infusions of plot and logic and coherence and propaganda and moralizing, and any other device that renders them more acceptable to the waking brain.

It's Monday evening, as dreary an evening as the day has been. We were expecting landscape gardeners to come and create order out of the wilderness of the back garden, but the rain has once more put them off. Richard Nixon became president today. I had a letter from Harry this morning, saying how much he is looking forward to coming over in May. 'It may sound mad to you, but thoughts of damp, dingy, broken-biscuit joys of collapsing Britain keep me working in sun-drenched California. There is no pleasing some people. . . .'

And I know that when we go over there for Christmas next December, I am looking forward to seeing the ruination of Mexico as much as the achievements of California.

When Chris Evans returns from the States, he wants me to appear on a panel with him to speak against telepathy; Koestler will speak for telepathy. An intimidating prospect, but a chance to meet Koestler.

Evans has an interesting refutation of telepathy on historical grounds. When the label 'telepathy' was coined in the 1880's, it must have held such a satisfyingly scientific ring that substantiation of its existence could lie only just round the corner. Research into telepathy was fathered by the same revolt against materialism that gave spiritualism such popularity. These were the weeds growing up round the grave of established religion.

This is how Evans concludes an article attacking telepathy and ESP in *The New Scientist*:

'Most striking, of course, is the way in which, to all but the totally committed, psychical research and its subject matter seem so hopelessly, woefully out of date; a relic of the past with an aura of faded pre-war newspapers, the Graf Zeppelin and the Entente Cordiale. What is really happening is that the old division of the universe into the "material" and the "spiritual", which has been with us for so long, has suddenly evaporated, and with it the very venerable belief that Man is an eternal and not a mortal being. For many centuries the psychic anecdote, the mystical experience, the supernatural power of evil and the insight of the prophet have all served to back up this belief and religion has taken this material for granted as part of its armoury. With the onslaught of science, however, hard facts were needed to back up religious dogma, and in a desperate battle many men, through spiritualism and psychical research and finally, when the screws were really being tightened, through parapsychology, attempted to produce these facts.

'That they have failed now seems increasingly certain. The long dream of Man's immortal nature is now ending, and we, whether we like it or not, are witnesses of the awakening.'

As Chris Evans says, the materialist basis of science, its desiccated nature of which Wells complains in his autobiography, forced many imaginative men to oppose it with some sort of supra-natural belief. Perhaps this is where Koestler stands. Now, the pendulum is swinging. Evans, once a believer in ESP, ceases to believe, and thus helps to counteract a prevalent tendency to believe in anything. No doubt in another generation it may be perfectly reasonable for his son to believe again. We all have to take in and throw out ballast to remain in equilibrium.

On that vital Wednesday when this book took me over, we talked about science fiction and Chris, as I have already reported, expressed his distaste for telepathy; he felt that writers were taking too easy a course in using it.

I have no objection to stories with telepathy in, provided they are worth reading on other counts. They then come under the second of C. S. Lewis's postulates as he sets them out in his essay *On Science Fiction*: 'a postulate which liberates consequences very far from comic, and, when this is so, if the story is good it will usually point a moral: of itself, without any didactic manipulation by the author on the conscious level.' Such a story is Walter Miller's *Command Performance*, a fine telepathy story, published in *Galaxy*, which I anthologized in the first *Penguin Science Fiction*.

9 Fifties SF and the Alien-As-Human

We have already talked about the sf of the forties, that almost secret *obbligato* to the disturbances of the war years. The sf of the fifties, when a great expansion of sf took place, was less hard-headed—less calculated, perhaps, to appeal to the engineers and blue-collar workers said to be the mainstay of *Astounding* readership.

One impression one sustains of the fifties is that there was too much telepathy. Stuck with nothing else to write about, a writer could always turn out a bit more telepathy. He could always turn out yet another story set on a spaceship, too, and, if he were really desperate, he could twist the tail and write a story of telepathy set on a spaceship!

Well, *plus ça change.* . . . I have recently been involved in correspondence in the SFWA *Bulletin* (SFWA being the Science Fiction Writers of America) about the over-use of such tired old inventions as the Faster-Than-Light drive, with which fictional spaceships are powered to get them rapidly to fictional solar systems. A few writers were irate because I pointed this out. In the latest edition of the *Bulletin*, one luckless writer tries to refute me by announcing—he is just writing a novel about telepathy set on a spaceship!

Without the power of imagination, sf is perpetually committed to this sort of treadmill. Normal people grow bored by the proliferation of robots and super-weapons and time-machines: though others are just as un-bore-able as the writers themselves! The result is a lot of conformity, with subsequent dearth of critical standards (poverty of scientific as well as literary qualities). Too much hardware, too great a lack of respect for the human software!

Sitting on the sofa with her feet up, Margaret reads this passage through and says, 'Hey, aren't you forgetting *Total Environment?*'

Total Environment is a novella of mine which she thinks well of. It concerns a certain empirical approach to the over-population problem.

'How does that connect?'

'*Total Environment* has telepathy in it; I know you always say consistency isn't your strong point, but you thought well enough of telepathy to use the idea then.'

'So I did!—I'd forgotten the telepathy bit. But without believing in it, just using telepathy as a postulate, I tried to create a situation that contained maximum potential for telepathy to develop. You know I had this idea that telepathy might be a sort of neurosis—a sickness in fact, rather than a strength, as it is usually thought to be.'

'The classical case of "hearing voices", in fact!'

'Maybe. We know that conditions of overcrowding produce neurosis, so in *Total Environment* I show telepathy emerging from a little overcrowded world.'

'All the same, you should take care what you say about not believing, and about there being too much telepathy.'

Good advice; I leave the passage in because this is not only a book but a book about becoming-a-book. (I also recall why I had forgotten about the elements of telepathy in *Total Environment*: because Hilary, admiring it, said that it would be even better if that strand of the story—which to him was superfluous—had been omitted; on reflection, I agree with him.)

Tuesday, 21st January. Telepathy apart, the expansionist science fiction of the fifties had much to commend it. Indeed, it was a little dazzling; it burst out of the confines of the forties when, as we have seen, it was virtually a secret movement; its context now was different: it was widely popular but still not accepted. This contrasts with the sixties situation, where, as reading matter, sf was perhaps slightly less popular than in the fifties, yet more widely accepted as a rational occupation for adult minds.

Having made such wide generalizations, I am forced to say that they can only represent overall patterns. One is partly in thrall to the mystique of numbers: to the notion that the forties must be different from the fifties and the fifties from the sixties, and so on. However, since everyone seems to be subject to this illusion to some extent, the illusion acquires some veracity: we are not at fault to speak of a *fin de siècle* feeling in the 1890's, even if the preoccupation with the death of the century was prompted by nothing more substantial than a leaf falling from the calendar.

Galaxy magazine began publication in the fall of 1950 and, within six months, *The Magazine of Fantasy and Science Fiction* was also on the stands. These two magazines, now old favourites, helped bring a more contemporary image to sf. *Galaxy*, for instance, took care to get creative interior illustrators like Emsh, Ashman and Sibley, while *F & SF* allowed no interior illustrations at all—a good idea when you saw the illustrations used by most of its rivals.

In those days, *Galaxy* was much to my taste. It is true that some of the stories that I sort-of-enjoyed then seem nauseatingly flip now; but there were serials, such as Pohl and Kornbluth's *Gravy Planet*, now known as *The Space Merchants*, and *Gladiator-at-Law*, and Alfred Bester's saga of Gully Foyle, *The Stars My Destination*, which appeared in book-form in England as *Tiger! Tiger!* I was so enthusiastic about the surrealist aspect of Bester's novel that his English publishers allowed me to write the copy of their advertisement for it free of charge!

Besides these and other individual excellences, each issue of *Galaxy* contained sufficiently varied sorts of stories for one to feel that the future was going to be varied and complex. This contrasted with *Astounding* in the forties, where a uniform business-like grimness made the future seem a bleak and simple place. The future may well be bleak, but it certainly shows no sign of becoming simple. Indeed, complexity is almost guaranteed, since it can be observed that new things do not always drive old things out, though they may drive them into corners. Things flourish in corners.

In this respect, prediction has often been wrong. As a child, I was told (or do I remember this only from hearsay?) that the spread of wireless would drive out the old Norfolk accent, so that everyone would speak BBC English. 'And a good job too!' said one adult severely.

When the talkies came along, we were told that American accents would drive out the old Norfolk accent. 'Disgraceful!' said several adults.

Only yesterday, we were told that TV would kill the reading habit. 'The end of literacy!' proclaimed an army of savants.

What actually happens is that the old things continue, perhaps in slightly diminished form, while new skills appear. Progressive Norfolk children learned more easily to pronounce their t's at school (dropping them again in the playground); later, they learned to do bad imitations of James Cagney; and now they read books and do homework while watching the Box.

Older patterns of behaviour persist tenaciously, in a culture as in an individual. They will yield, and make way for the new; but not at once, and not entirely. Even the English have taken to central heating at last; but I fancy many families are like ours: we turn the radiators off in the bedrooms last thing at night and open the windows. It's more than public school training coming out. We need the new: we need the old.

In America, I know, these things are differently arranged. But the Americans have good historical reasons for regarding both their land and their culture as new, so that the old traditions are not there to fall back on to the same extent. Whether you think this a good or bad state of affairs is a matter for individual temperament.

When Margaret and I stayed with James and Judy Blish on Riverside Drive, our desire for open windows at night caused our hosts some inconvenience, and led to the eventual escape of some of their cats down the fire escape. (Even Kaikabod was soon recovered.)

The future promises increasing complexity. Our happiness and fulfilment lie in maintaining a double attitude: in recognizing and enjoying the innate feeling of simplicity towards all things which can come if one has clear goals, goals not in conflict with one's basic make-up, and in recognizing and enjoying the enormous complexity of being of which we are a part.

In the early fifties, at least one new theme emerged from the conspiracy of science fiction writers, a theme that epitomizes the fears and complications of the age better than all the vast output of space-fiction. This was the theme used, *mutatis mutandis*, in Ray Bradbury's story in *The Martian Chronicles* (*The Silver Locusts* in Britain) called *The Third Expedition*; in Alan Nourse's *Counterfeit*; and in two stories by Philip K. Dick, *Colonist* and *Impostor*: the alien-as-human theme.

The idea is that something with evil intentions, preferably an alien being, can take on the outward semblance of humanity to further its ambitions. It effects this transformation either by shape-changing, or by imposing its disguise direct on to the minds of real humans.

In the Bradbury story, the alien manages its satanic chameleonism by powerful telepathy. One sees immediately that such a theme goes right back to myth; Leda and the swan is a perennially popular example. This is less a token of the theme's lack of originality than proof of its imaginative strength; although one must add that it also harks back to the primitive dualist belief in evil as an external force, a lapse to which science fiction is particularly prone. Nevertheless, in this fifties handling, the alien-as-human theme is used anti-dualistically, as far as that is possible.

The Nourse story (which, after I had anthologized it in one of my Penguin collections, was turned into a television play) makes it clear that the alien who is returning to Earth in human guise is not only (a) up to no good at all, as is shown by the insidious cunning of its disguise, but (b) is almost indistinguishable from a man by anything but the most rigorous scientific analyses. Even microscopic examination of the alien's tissues will not serve to penetrate its monstrous disguise. Nourse is saying, in other words, that we could be pure evil and even our best friends would not tell us from good—until too late.

Dick takes this line of speculation a step further in *Impostor*.

Incidentally, here is a case where the incestuous nature of the sf field acts to its advantage. When the alien-as-human theme was popular in the early fifties, not only plagiarism was at work: the authors were conducting a dialogue through their stories on matters that interested them.

Dick's *Impostor* appeared in 1953, a year after *Counterfeit*. By a masterly stroke, Dick switches the evil, from remote threat on spaceship, into vivid close-up. Is Oldham the innocent man he believes himself to be, or a complex android with a nuclear weapon inside him, deposited on Earth by aliens to usurp the real Oldham's place and destroy his project? Oldham himself does not know the answer! This is a marked gain over earlier appearances of the theme, in that it corresponds much more closely to both ancient and contemporary views of psychology: we deceive ourselves and

the truth is not in us. (Incidentally *Impostor* is an early example
of Dick's preoccupation with 'Real versus Fake'.)

The alien-as-human dialogue continued. In 1954, Frederik
Pohl's *The Tunnel Under the World* appeared. Unlike Dick, Pohl
is not greatly interested in problems of good and evil; social
questions are his forte, and so it transpires in *Tunnel*, where
Burckhardt is a victim of ruthless advertising methods. All the
same, Pohl does not neglect certain ontological aspects of Burckhardt's case, and many of the frissons of the plot derive from the
same uncertainty as to his 'real' nature that troubled Oldham. Here
I think one might say that the original impulse behind this theme
is slackening; Pohl is constrained to pile on the ingenuities. While
sf is, among many other things, a literature of ingenuity, so is
Practical Mechanics, and extra complications generally represent
a dwindling of the imaginative impulse.

Not that the idea was dead. In 1955, in the English magazine
New Worlds, a new author called Brian Aldiss appeared with a
story entitled *Outside*, again on the alien-as-human theme. I was
interested in the way that the impostors would be imprisoned by
their own cleverness, as the first line of the story intimates: 'They
never went out of the house.'

It happens that we can observe how this story and its theme
struck readers outside the sf field. In his wide-ranging book, *The
Strength to Dream*, Colin Wilson says this: 'In a story of less than
five thousand words, Mr. Aldiss has succeeded in creating an
effective symbol of the human condition and posing the problem
"Who am I?" in a new and startling way. . . . All the same, it
should be noted that some of Aldiss's themes appear elsewhere.'

You bet they do! One of the limitations of the sf field is that
one is never quite an independent voice, but always has to walk
under an umbrella, even when the rain has stopped.

Wilson goes on to mention two predecessors to *Outside*, one
being Dick's *Impostor*, and the other van Vogt's *The Sound*, which
appeared in *Astounding* in 1950. He might have mentioned Eric
Frank Russell's *Metamorphosite* of 1946. He might equally have
mentioned that the 1960 Christmas issue of *The Spectator*—not
quite the magazine one immediately looks to when searching for
sf—carried a science fiction story by Kingsley Amis called *Something Strange*, in which the alien-as-human theme reappeared.

And so one might go on, back and forth, seeking antecedents and successors. New thinking can always bring forth an old idea in fresh form. It may well have been the disgust at ourselves, following the discovery of what a civilized nation like Germany could do to its supposed enemies, which gave this obsession with evil-that-is-not-us-yet-of-us such a powerful new lease of life.

10   Piranesi Unchained

Wednesday, 22nd January. Not the best day for concentrated work! Motors roar outside the house; our landscape gardeners have arrived at last! Timothy stands with his nose to the window as tractors and shovels and rotavators and trucks grind to and forth. Of course, it began to rain within an hour or two of their arrival.

My new secretary appeared this morning and made a business-like approach to typewriter and dictaphone, but neither of us managed to get through a great deal of work. We wrote a letter to John Brunner, who has taken on his shoulders much of the organization of this year's Easter science fiction convention in Oxford.

I gave myself yesterday afternoon off, and Margaret and I drove in to Oxford with Timothy, to set me up in stationery for today's grand opening event, and to call in on my mother. Mother was in cheerful spirits—the mild winter has worked to her advantage. We took her some early daffodils still in bud. She strolled to the gate with us afterwards, taking pleasure in pointing out her bulbs springing up.

We bought a Piranesi print in Oxford—in Sanders', where I worked when I first came to Oxford looking for a job. We smuggled it home later, not liking Mama to see that we had been extravagant; it was only just after Christmas that we bought an Alma-Tadema.

This engraving is not one of Piranesi's marvellous metaphysical prisons, but one of his views of Rome in ruins: the mausoleum of Helen, mother of the Emperor Constantine, fallen into a comfortable decay, with ferns and bushes sprouting from every coign and corner. In the middle of this lapsed grandeur, an eighteenth-century villa has been built.

When I first went to work at Sanders', the old man had a splendid collection of prints and rare books stashed away on his shelves. He was a frustrated book-collector, and must have owned fifteen or sixteen copies of Ackermann's *Repository of Oxford* alone! And in one corner of the print room, he kept a huge shallow wooden box, which contained giant Piranesi engravings—the credible hells of the *Carceri*.

That grim first flowering of Romanticism! How it impressed me! Sanders had a dark set of the engravings, selling for a modest price. I wish I could have afforded them then, in 1949; but I was being paid only three pounds a week, and could not even settle my laundry bills without my father's assistance.

For living with, the views of Rome are more comfortable than the prisons. The one we bought will hang in the dining-room when Mama leaves—and when I have finished redecorating the room. One hardly needs reminding, however splendidly, of the gloom of the human condition, over food and wine designed to banish that gloom!

Thursday, 23rd January. Whatever else one might say about Mr. Sanders, he certainly acquired some beautiful books and paintings. In his own collection, he had some landscapes by Thomas Rowlandson very far removed from that master's gross style; these landscapes were almost chaste, yet with a hint of that peculiarly luxurious Rowlandsonian line. They showed plain countrysides and deserted beaches, decorated occasionally with a sweet Georgian maiden, buxom and witty, as only Rowlandson could manage. Those watercolours were not copies but abstracts of landscapes, with a calligraphic quality that one finds echoed in the early Michael Ayrton. It's amazing to me that the rumpus of William Blake is always with us, yet magnificent Rowlandson never quite comes into his own. Perhaps it is because his achievements, unlike Blake's, cannot be appreciated in reproduction.

I'd collect Rowlandson if I had enough money. He was not a great artist in the world's hierarchy, because he never transcended his nationality; yet in that limitation lies much of his appeal. He is English, and reminds us of and laughs at our own Englishness. He would be a good choice to hang in Heath House. They had Buffet on the walls before we moved in! Buffet!

This is a light and airy house. G. B. Tiepolo would look well here too. The Ashmolean has one or two attractive Tiepolo paintings, and Margaret and I have seen him in his full mature glory in the frescoes at the palace in Würzburg; but what I modestly covet are some of his etchings!

Tiepolo was the last of the great Venetian painters to whom the gods or genes gave the gift of depicting the human figure as if it was of more transcendent importance than the grand architecture surrounding it. He was a contemporary of Piranesi; I met them cheek-by-jowl in the crowded little rooms of Sanders' shop.

Sanders had some of the *Capricci* and *Scherzi*, Tiepolo's two great series of etchings. Tiepolo is no more like Piranesi than I to Hercules. He is all light and air; his buildings, instead of imprisoning, serve as mere foils for the human drama; his humans, even in repose, have life and movement—whereas Piranesi's figures, even in movement, are stunned with some unhallowed inertia. One is Ariel, one Caliban. Caliban has his power and Ariel his magic. The *Scherzi* (and they would be my choice) are full of magic.

I don't remember them very well, not having seen them for years except in reproduction, but I know the subject was—in the lightest and most breakfast-table of ways—enchantment, quest, ruination, death. Enigmatic animals appear. Groups of fine-looking people and old men stand together, scarcely speaking. Punchinello is disinterred from his grave. On a shattered hillside littered with the trophies of war, a man stands in meditation with his back to us. There are snakes, and, virtually Tiepolo's trademark, a shattered pine.

If I were editing a science fiction magazine (which God forbid!), or a magazine of speculative fiction as our stomachs prefer the term nowadays, I would run the *Scherzi* as covers. They would have immense appeal, the magazine would sell out, and I'd be left with a fine set of etchings!

It has taken me a day's labour to set down these thoughts, which flashed through my head while our Piranesi was being wrapped up—well, I say flashed: but the experts have discovered the speed of thought to be a mere 225 miles per hour. Which means I must be living at the rate of twenty rods, poles or perches per second!

Another thought crossed my mind at the same time, and I determined to write it down here. The Piranesi we bought—it relates to my dream of comfort! My dream is a highly coloured parody of the Piranesi! The villa inside Helen's mausoleum was bowdlerized by my dream into the cottage inside the ruined church. . . . I am full of astonishment at the discovery.

It was before Christmas that I first looked at the Piranesi and decided I could not afford it, and did not like two small foxing marks on it. That was before I contemplated this book, and at a time when I had not thought of my dream for a long while.

Coincidence! Or more than coincidence?

So there arises the lure that beckons all simple philosophers: to reduce all diversity to a single strand! It can be done like this. I liked the Piranesi, not because it reminded me of the comforting dream, but because both dream and picture have their sources in a common impulse.

This simple explanation is one calculated to appeal to my temperament. From the old and grand and ruinous grows a new thing; arguments can readily be adduced in favour of both old and new, and these arguments originate from different sides of my personality. On behalf of the old, the conservationist side of me says that what is old is fine and must not be edited out or destroyed, while the new is a poor lesser thing, parasitic, and in some respects a desecration. On behalf of the new, the progressive side of me says that only from the new can anything worthwhile originate—even the old *began* new—and that the old must be treated as speculative capital or else it is dead weight.

And, the argument of reduction continues triumphantly, this also accounts for your attraction to the concept of the neocortex wrapped thinly round the old limbic brain. The symbols are the same. Your own life, your own books, are similar spurts of the new bursting from the old.

In itself, all this argument may not be untrue. Only in its pretensions towards being the whole truth is it totally untrue.

The reduction of human beings to diagrams no longer attracts me (which is part of my quarrel with sf, where men operate on such simplificative circuits). I will bring my Piranesi home and hang it (when Mama has gone!) and be content to enjoy it for itself.

/

11 An SF Convention in the Fifties

When I first came downstairs this morning, at 8.15, it was still scarcely daylight. Mist pressed thickly up against the house. As I took the chain off the front door, I could see car headlights down on the road flitting like will-o'-the-wisps beyond the invisible tree-trunks. I moved through the house, drawing curtains, not putting on any lights for as long as possible, trying to persuade Nickie to go out for her morning pee.

The intense love one has of one's home is really a love of life itself. At the time, I believed we would never be more content anywhere than we were at Jasmine. Yet we are as content, or more so, here. That pokey house at Kidlington was the only one I felt little affection for; my terraced house in Marston Street was smaller, yet I loved it. Were I put in solitary confinement for a term of years, I would grow to love every miserable stone of my cell!

Now we battle with the County Planners for the right to live here undisturbed.

In the confinement of my study, let me get back to the subject of science fiction in the fifties, when we were very young.

The name of Philip K. Dick has already been mentioned. He emerged with a great burst of activity in the early fifties, and has kept up a hefty output ever since. Perhaps because he is too facile, the actual quality of his writing is sometimes shoddy. This is a criticism often levelled at the greatest novelists—Dickens and Dostoevsky notably. But Dick is a man obsessed by a great theme; it is hard, as it should be, to outline exactly what this theme is, although it has to do with basics like the equations of evil and the obsessive quality of life and the struggle between real and false.

In his best books, Dick stays within this great glowing target area and achieves some remarkable hits.

It is in this quality of pursuing a theme that Dick is able to rise above his fellows; the heavy guns of Robert Heinlein, the intelligent little cages of Robert Sheckley, the joyous disasters of John Wyndham, cannot compare with that peculiar Dick mixture of utter madness and sheer sanity interfused in novels like *Martian Timeslip*, *The Three Stigmata of Palmer Eldritch*, *Do Androids Dream Electric Sheep?* and the superb *Man in the High Castle*.

Of other writers active in the early fifties, the first name to burst like a starshell from the SF ghetto was Ray Bradbury. His introduction into England was distinguished. Rupert Hart-Davis recognized the quality of his writing and published him in elegant hard-cover editions. The *Observer* published some of his short stories. It was a curious sensation to open the Sunday paper and find there Bradbury's *Golden Apples of the Sun*, illustrated by Leonard Rosoman. The last time that story had appeared was in *Startling Stories*, behind a lurid cover which would have killed off the sensitive readers of the *Observer*!

In those (comparatively) early days, science fiction won some excellent supporters. They largely succeeded in their aim of securing for science fiction a civilized level of readership and, as a result of their efforts, I believe that science fiction enjoys better attention in this country than in America—ironical really, since America is its true home, and Wells's lusty infant was adopted and suckled in New York. I have already mentioned Kingsley Amis and Edmund Crispin (Bruce Montgomery), who were readers of sf in and before their Oxford days, and went on to fight for its recognition as tolerable reading matter. There were also Angus Wilson and Marghanita Laski, both respected names by the mid-fifties, who worked through the *Observer* to get sf accepted. When the paper ran a competition for a story set in the year A.D. 2500, I had the good fortune to find my story, *Not for an Age*, printed in the paper one Sunday. That was only a couple of months after Faber & Faber had published my first book; my career was launched at last!

Faber at that time was carrying a small sf list, when most of the other London publishers had abandoned the genre (that some abandoned it only temporarily was partly due to Faber's stalwart example). They had brought out the first of Crispin's *Best SF* anthologies in great style, and some of James Blish's novels—all of which received respectful critical attention. But science fiction is really no very strange thing to the British temperament, nor am I the first writer of fantasy to emerge from Oxford. (Carroll, art thou sleeping there below?)

My first published book was a comedy and not science fiction. When Charles Monteith asked what I intended to do next, I replied, tentatively, that I was writing sf stories. 'Absolutely splendid,' Charles wrote back. 'Just what we are looking for.'

I could not have found a better publisher. Fabers brought out my first story collection, *Space Time and Nathaniel*, in 1957 and my first novel *Non-Stop* (which was called *Starship* in the States, to my dismay) the year after. In those days, it was very difficult to get sf published in a decent hard-cover edition, and almost as difficult in paperback.

Not until 1957 did I enter the somewhat amazing family life of sf, the clannish world of fandom which looks so ambivalently on the mundane world and often fails to see that, like the mundane world, it also is composed of destructive as well as constructive elements. Nobody has written an intelligent book about fandom; it would be well worth reading; but the author would surely be crowned with thorns!

The grand occasion in 1957 was the holding of the World Science Fiction Convention in London—the first time this annual event had been allowed to stray outside the North American continent—thanks mainly to the efforts of an Anglophile American fan, Dave Kyle. Dave married Ruth Landis, and they flew over to London as part of their honeymoon. That honeymoon feeling was infectious.

Was that nondescript year really 1957, and not 1947? The convention was held in a terrible hotel in the Queensway district. A distinctly post-war feeling lingered. Bomb damage was still apparent. Was sugar still rationed? It can't have been, but there was no mistaking the general American recoil from the ghastliness of plumbing and food, and their amazement at the prostitutes parading along the Bayswater Road! The whores had not adjusted their make-up to the new sodium lighting, and looked as if they could offer mankind nothing better than necrophilia.

An SF Convention of the Fifties

Timorous new writer, I knew before I reached the convention that I should never have gone, that it would not be my *métier*. I fell in with an English fan who was an old hand at these occasions, and we headed for the hotel together.

'You've got some pep pills?'

'No,' I said.

'You'll need pep pills. Got to keep awake somehow! You'll get no sleep at a con, believe you me Kettering.'

'You surprise me.'

'At Kettering last year, nobody in the whole hotel got any sleep for the entire weekend beer!'

'What's that?'

'Beer. I never saw so much beer consumed in all my life. You like beer?'

'I can take it.'

'You'd better! Stick by me, you'll be all right!'

I lost him in the foyer of the hotel, but he caught me again as I was tiptoeing down from my room.

'There you are! It's going to be hell. Don't be nervous. Are you feeling hungry talk?'

'What?'

'Talk! We'll be talking all night! Ken Slater's got his stall up, Ron Bennett's checked in and the fans are kneeling round Walt Willis already Ghod.'

'Walt Willis is Ghod?'

'You believe it too? That's what the fans say. It annoys Walt. We'd better go and get a bite to eat. I know a good place to go. There won't be another chance unless we fill up well now. Yes, they call him Ghod.'

I trudged along with my new-found friend, knowing that I would never make the grade in his high-tension world, knowing that the great Willis would instinctively reject (and that with a pun) any clumsy genuflections I might attempt. As my friend regaled me with heroic tales of other cons, of drunken laughter, of awful Chinese meals, of fights with zap-guns, of bottles dropped from roofs down hotel-managers' chimneys, of old ladies complaining, of young ladies losing precious possessions, of mini-cons held (hilariously, of course, always hilariously) in baths full of cold water, realization crept—stamped, indeed—over me that in the

101

great three-day sorting that was about to overtake the world, my shortcomings as to clubbability would be pitifully revealed.

My worldly friend and I marched into a small Greek restaurant in Queensway.

'Should be someone worth talking to in here,' said my friend loudly, looking round.

In the shadiest corner, a man and woman sat at a table. Both were toying with dishes of lukewarm food. She was smoking, with blurred lazy movements of her wrist. They were talking to each other in quiet voices.

'Told you, I told you!' exclaimed my friend, hurrying over to them. As I followed, he said—to me, to them, to the whole mundane restaurant, 'It's Forry, the Great 4E! How are you, Forry, remember me, remember Kettering, remember that comic taxi driver? This is Mr. Science Fiction, Forrest Ackermann, you must have heard of him! I was just reading your column in *Nebula*, Forry. There are some great sf films coming along, by what you say.'

'Hollywood's doing its best for us,' Forry said, smiling. His spectacles flashed in my direction. 'And won't you introduce us?'

'Oh, yes, I forgot, this is Brian Aldiss.'

'Brian *W.* Aldiss?' asked Forry.

Nothing has ever sounded more courteous to my ears. There was no bluster to Forry. He is one of the few men who has attended all the world science fiction conventions; since he was a spotty youth, he fought to help sf establish itself; and he has built up one of the world's largest private collections of sf; but none of this you learn from Forry.

We sat down with him and Mary. I believe I did have something to eat. I know I became completely under their spell, as the empathy started working overtime. My worldly friend disappeared somewhere along the line in search of other celebrities. Forry, Mary and I just sat and talked. Later, we strolled back to the hotel and met Val and Lee and other members of the entourage, and Dave and Ruth. I remained with them for most of the con, while the band played 'Dirty Old Town'.

So I saw little of other new writers who were present. I do remember John Brunner; at an incredibly early age, he seemed to

be running everything. Most people begin sf activities scanda-
lously young. Ted Carnell, then editor of *New Worlds*, who had
advised me to write *Non-Stop*, ushered me into a bar where a press
conference was being held and John Brunner was telling the
reporters what was what. I do not recall that any of the reporters
spoke to me.

I went to the bar and bought a drink. Standing next to me was
a slim young man who told me that there were some extraordinary
types at the convention, and that he was thinking of leaving pretty
smartly. He introduced himself as J. G. Ballard. I had already read
his early short stories in *New Worlds*; indeed, at that time, his were
the only short stories (apart from my own) that I could read there
with any pleasure.

A month or two before the convention, *Astounding* had published a novelette with the irresistible title of *The Stainless Steel
Rat*. Its author, Harry Harrison, was my age and already had a
solid history of sf-activity, including the editing of a professional
magazine. With the payment from *Stainless Steel Rat*, and an
adventurous optimism entirely typical of him, Harry bought air
tickets for himself and his wife and son, and came over to live in
Europe, where he stayed for several years. I hardly remember him
at the convention; there remains only a vision of him and Joan
chasing an infant and highly mobile Toddy down one of the
hotel's macabre corridors.

The big guns were also present at that convention. Guest of
Honour was John W. Campbell, one of the most influential men
in magazine sf. I saw him talking gravely to Eric Frank Russell,
whose laconic humour made him one of my admired writers. John
Wyndham was there, gentlemanly and quiet as ever amid the
mêlée; and Robert Abernathy, an excellent writer; and Arthur C.
Clarke, who flew over from Ceylon to dazzle us with a few tricks
from his magic briefcase; and the all-knowing and genial Sam
Moskowitz, who even today fights valiantly for the kind of fiction
he read and enjoyed as a boy.

Oh, and many more, as the memory splutters faultily into life.
I find my Evans-Newman de-programming system did a fairly
thorough job on that convention. Ken and Pamela Bulmer, very
gay; an Irish writer, James White, dashing about firing zap-guns
at people; John Christopher, who gave me good advice which I

actually took, and whose brilliant novel, *Death of Grass*, made the London of those days seem even more dangerous than it was; John Boland, who was yet to write *League of Gentlemen*, and had produced a nice catastrophe, *White August*; Robert Silverberg, looking even younger then than now; a chubby and smiling young man called Tom Boardman Jnr., whose publishing firm was bringing out some good hard-core sf. And many other young giants, no doubt, for the times they were a-changing!

12   How I Ran Through An Empire – And Was Better For It

As a solitary individual, I never belonged to any company but the motley company of sf-dom. Among the nutcases are many people who find no niche elsewhere, and who have a real if untutored interest in the many subjects on which sf fringes—chief among which is, I take it, the vital question of how life might be improved, and what exactly mankind thinks he is making of his life.

Where many are deluded is in believing that a proliferation of machines and technology improves life's quality. That idea was exposed long ago—by John Ruskin, for one instance, who was aware of what still remains the modern paradox: that the machine, being destructive of creativity and spontaneous values, threatens the inner life (it is this threat that contemporary art, by advancing towards the machine-principle, seeks to oppose); while, as far as outer life is concerned, the machine has managed no better than the slaves it replaces to create plenty for everyone—'the essence of wealth consists in power over man'. All this is in Ruskin's *Unto This Last*, published in 1860, but the preponderant belief in sf circles is, I am sure, the reverse of this.

Together with this technologically based optimism goes a deep conservatism, which shows itself in two ways in science fiction: in the way that posited Americas—even those set several centuries into the future, with complete automation and maybe complete telepathy and space travel—are still but thinly veiled versions of today's capitalist West. The old order changeth not. We may be lording it over a thousand galactic races, but none of their culture ever seeps back here and the old greenback democracy still incredibly flourishes. Conservatism and the fears behind it produce this failure of the imagination.

The other way in which conservatism shows is in an almost frantic fight to retain old forms of fiction and even the old subjects —forms and subjects not exactly fresh when pulp sf began in 1926! So the ostensibly forward-looking is often the backward-looking.

These tendencies are more apparent in the States than England at present. The last-ditchers—with Sam Moskowitz possibly producing most decibels on their behalf—are noisier, or perhaps just of better calibre, there. Understandably. In this country, you don't have to be middle-aged yet to have seen enormous changes— the complete dissolution of an empire, no less, a process one might have expected to take centuries which was packed into a few years. We are readier to accept change as a constant in our daily lives. So American sf has no equivalent of *1984*, or of the more venturesome speculative novels in which category I would like to think my own *Report On Probability A* and *Barefoot in the Head* belong.

Education for change will have to be built into future teaching programmes. Possibly one of the best educations for change we have at present is the forward-looking science fiction.

Scientific advances can be full of drama and excitement to a sophisticated audience; yet science, we are told, appeals rather less to the young than it did.

If this is the case, it is because science has become entangled with the very forces that once (say in Wells's youth) it opposed. The young are beginning to see science as part of the massive barrier confronting youth, as a tool of oppression. Like God, technology is on the side of the big battalions.

The space race, technology's big circus, hammers the lesson home. The space race with all the meaningless national prestige involved—is a flight from humanity's pressing problems. This is the gravest indictment against it.

Already, it's a middle-aged dream, yet another evasion of reality.

One views events through the lessons of one's own upbringing. In the thirties, the vision of the future (meaning the sixties and seventies) which drew me was of shining towers. And what did we get instead? Wandsworth! Unpalatable mish-mash of old and modern, encased in increasingly sterile formulae! Poor Wandsworth, thou shouldst be living at this hour!

It is still possible to believe that the goal of true science could be to free men's minds rather than enslave them. To free them from superstition, if the limbic brain will allow.

Let's hope that inventions like the ward, one's personal hot-line to the world's facts, will free us from many old structures and allow new generations new time to live new lives. We still live essentially Victorian lives; newer, freer patterns are latent only.

It's too late in this day for me to think constructively. I return to here and now, sit at the desk over a cigar and gin-and-Campari. We brought the Campari duty-free from Malta. How long will all that duty-free nonsense persist, token of nationalities and barriers? It is too hard to imagine a time when nationalities have dissolved, or when Croats and Serbs, Flems and Walloons, Catholics and Protestants, have forgotten those labels.

Monday, 27th January. Nothing written here since last Thursday. Subliminal time flows between one entry and the next.

As children, when we had to go to Church every Sunday, we were given little stamp albums to fill with bright sentimental stamps, one for each Sabbath's attendance, rather like Green Shield stamps. In the empty squares stood the following jingle:

> Every stamp says 'Duty Done',
> Every blank cries 'Shame'!
> Finish what you have begun
> In the Saviour's name. . . .

Such things stick, like an advertising jingle, and a lingering neolithic idiot in the head beats time to them.

How I Ran Through An Empire—And Was Better For It

We have been too busy here for me to get to the typewriter. Apart from my weekly review (this time, I had Professor Hyne's *The Edwardian Turn of Mind*, which I reviewed both for the *Oxford Mail* and *New Worlds*), we had Margaret's cousin Margot to stay with us for the weekend. All I can present here is our little private sector moving on.

In the public world, great events are in process, the more portentous because we are unable to view them in perspective.

Jan Palach, the twenty-one-year-old Czech student, burnt himself in Prague, as a protest against Russian occupation and censorship.

President Nixon has taken office.

In the technical/scientific sphere, Soviet cosmonauts have linked together two *Soyuz* vehicles to form the first crude spacestation, and an American team has synthesized an enzyme for the first time. From either of these last two events, a host of predictions are possible; for better or worse, we have come appreciably nearer, in just the last three weeks, to reaching the stars and creating artificial life!

My sister has sent me a cutting about the prevalence of moulds, fungi and bacteria living on human skin. It appears that in well-frequented areas like armpit and crutch, the average bacteria population is about two and a half million per square centimetre. Faced with this evidence of life's proliferation, how can we doubt that planets of other stars are swarming with life? What are the prolix histories of the populations of your upper leg?

It's evening now. Almost no work done all day, although there were admittedly interruptions. The biggest interruption was the fine weather. When Margaret and her mother were in town with Timothy, I put on my gum-boots and went out. I cultivated my garden. Now, after supper, the moon is shining brightly, Venus is riding along the sky, and all is still. A Tiepolo magic fills the sight, while Punchinello Spring lies only just below ground.

On the other days, I have worked like a slave. Everybody should be able to work as I do: when they please, with a rhythm dictated by interest rather than necessity. J. B. Priestley once pointed out the artificiality of the nine-to-five routine, five or six days a week, fifty weeks a year. I couldn't do it any more. I work with great industry—in fits and starts. When you have children, the *bourgeoise* life closes inevitably down—there's nothing so middle-class as kids—and hours have to become more regular; but I still work during day and evening as fancy suits me. My desk is a pleasurable place. I've seen an empire collapse: I keep working pretty regularly.

Some of my writer friends gear themselves to systems that militate against good work. They wait till a crisis blows up: the brokers are at the door, the wife threatens to leave, the electricity is cut off. Then they shut themselves in a room with a typewriter and thrash out a novel in four or five days, nourished only by a bottle of whisky or coffee brought in by a tiptoeing mistress.

Anthony Powell, on the other hand, writes only one thousand words a day. I imagine a private income makes a writer more secure. Anthony Burgess, one of the most human and enjoyable of today's British writers, has been one of the most industrious. Now he is in Malta, and may be able to take life easier, away from the greedy British tax man.

I ought to write a book about writers. Most of them have more troubles than I. The truth is, I live on the edge of a whole little scene of writers and readers of which nothing is generally known. When I'm old and even more garrulous than now, I'll write that book.

Often, these days, I catch myself believing that I am more fortunate than most of my fellow writers, in circumstances if not in talent. Let's hope that they feel the same. Happiness is not exclusive—after all, both British and French managed to celebrate the Battle of Trafalgar as a victory over their enemies. . . .

13   A Perfect Posited Image of This Book

Tuesday, 28th January. It is now a long trail winding back to the Wednesday when the Evanses were here. Since Chris left for the States, the aura of crisis which *New Worlds* always wears has sharpened. Charles Platt, Mike Moorcock, Jimmy Ballard and I—we've been ringing each other, flying a few distress signals. Charles is coming down at the weekend, and will meet Peter Guy; it is just possible that his student publishing group might help to produce the magazine.

No, it's more than a magazine. It's Mike's lifeblood, it's a social focus, it's a microcosmic part of history. It's also a part of the only really live and life-giving fiction being written today.

The fact that we all suffer desperately from general bloody neglect is neither here nor there—or rather it's here, because if commercial success were all that was at stake, we'd be elsewhere. In twenty years time, of course, *New Worlds* will be a roaring commercial success, and collectors will be fighting for tatty old issues, to read every precious word we wrote. Other firms will reprint it and make a bomb. We'll be part of the wallpaper then. The world is twenty years behind the times.

Look at this book—fumbling, staggering, groping, but trying to equate the human thing with the mammoth-escalator thing. When I wrote my first travel book, *Cities and Stones*, I knew at the end of it that I had then learnt how to write a travel book. My second would be better if I found the right country. I've never had time to write a second. When I've finished this book, I'll have learnt to write speculative layer-cake or whatever you like to call this recipe (I picture it like a TV set sunk into a ball of batter, burnt at the edges, soft in the centre, being hurled ahead . . . who knows where it will land).

But I'll never write a second book like this. (Not that it is original in form; there was Jacquetta Hawkes's *A Land*, which I have read twice and much admire—a fine science-fictional sensibility at work!) With every novel I write, I grasp something, and then don't wish to repeat it; there's always something else to do. I'm longing to write my play. I'm full of ideas. The days aren't long enough. Nor do I see enough people. All sorts of people I want to talk to I never talk to for lack of time.

Anthony Burgess was complaining of the way authors subsidize their own calling by writing at low rates for such sources as *The Times Literary Supplement*, and said he was going to stop doing so. I should stop too, give up this subsidizing publishers and the Westminster Press by spending a considerable number of hours

each week reviewing for peanuts! Yet it gets in the bloodstream;
like sleep, it has to be undergone. Also, reviewing helps you keep
abreast of things, as they say. Good God, I could have read six
books on Ché Guevara last year alone—for nothing!

Publishers. . . . I hope Peter Guy's publishing course will
produce revolutionaries, Chés of Printing House Square! Elizabeth and her friends . . . will they make a book look like a modern
object? I'd like to see this book produced as a coffee-table book.
Why not? Gather into it the kipple (is there such a word as 'kipple'
in the States, or did Phil Dick invent it especially for *Do Androids
Dream Electric Sheep?*)—the kipple of these days, photographs of
the cigar-butts on my desk, stubbed in my glass ashtray with that
proud legend stamped large on it: N.A.A.F.I. HONG KONG; shots of
the study itself; the shelves of books; the big blow-ups on the
walls (*SF Horizons*); the Piranesi standing on the floor against
Harry's battered old ex-Army filing-cabinet; Clive's drawings;
the prototype for the jacket of *An Age* or the paperback edition
of *The Airs of Earth* which called me 'Britain's Premier Science
Fiction Writer' just to rattle Arthur; shots of stairs, banisters,
angles, verticals restful and strict with the vision, the enormous
fertilizing power of dull light on low ceiling, the deserts of fitted
carpet; I'm alone in the house at present and every room is silent,
particularly the living-room where Nickie sprawls and sleeps; I
must get the place fitted up with omnivision, as in *Still Trajectories*, so that I can sit here and enjoy the sight and sound of
the silences in every room, each silence distinct and particular,
like treed calf on this floor, various scents of elder on the floor
below, like a marble surface on the ground floor, except for the
living-room which is twiggy with its huge windows, and the rear
kitchen where the silence is drawn up from a black eighteenth-
century well; yes, it's precious—how marvellous it must be on
Mars today about lunchtime, with not a thing stirring up the
centuries except those minute rupicolous xxizyzipedes, two and a
half million to every square centimetre; and endless endless photographs of all our trees by day and by night, blurred shots, enough
to drive a book-buyer round the bend; a pocket in the back of the
book containing genuine twigs, signed and numbered; Margaret's
face; her hair; the especial cyclonic contours of her skull; and, if
you want photos of me, the bizarre one by Jerry Bauer used on

the back of the Four Square edition of *Earthworks*, with one side of my face all enlightened and benevolent and blank, and the other like a Dalian canker, submerged into hypogeal shadow—that superimposed on to the façade of Heath House, which supports the same schizophrenia; pages plastered with images of our drinks cupboard, a treasury of fifty shots of our cellar, the downstairs lavatory with its two shitters, one for tiny tots; views of the ravaged garden, close-ups that would make mountains of the molehills; faces of Henry Miller all mandarin, and Sir Thomas Browne's disinterred skull, stills from *Last Year in Marienbad*, a photograph of Harry's photo of me photographing Harry in Primošten; dead leaves from the big Spanish chestnuts which still invade our side passage (they live in the hedges and bide their time); pictures of Tony Luke, the post-lady, the newspaper man, Timothy roaring with laughter, Timothy howling with sorrow, Timothy sleeping with his Teddy, Timothy setting off down the drive towards eternity; my shoes; the courtyard; facsimiles of notes in my notebook: 'James Joyce. Oddity of his conversation. Spoke only of parakeets to Le Corbusier and of headaches and truffles to Proust. With Dwight MacDonald and George L. K. Morris, he spoke only of the price and size of latter's apartment'; photographs of pages of numbers; illos from *New Worlds*, shots of my friends—Bon, Tony, Jon, Harry, Hilary, Charles, Jannick, *et al.*, *et al.*; copies of some of my better reviews—make the whole thing like a scrapbook—when I landed at Copenhagen airport a couple of years ago, I was asked by Jannick Storm, 'Nobody is here to meet you, no photographers or press men—how does it feel to be an unknown celebrity?'; the book could put over what it feels like; I'd even take most of the shots myself, just to keep down Faber's costs—unknown celebrities are like that!; and bits of old manuscripts, maybe shuffled a bit to give them edge; I'm sure that my Acid Head novel, *Barefoot in the Head*, is going to be great (and recognized as such when I'm in a bathchair or whatever people do nowadays instead of bathchairs—marry a fifth time, I guess!)— but I would like to see a shuffled version produced at the same time; it might possess extra voltage; Faber got the printer to do a little four-page prospectus of *Barefoot* to see how things went, and they ran the first page, a middle page, and a page of concrete poems together; the resultant variable geography does have a charge all its own; well, that prospectus must go in; photograph of my publisher, of course, to keep him sweet, perhaps the two of us in All Souls or, no, the one of him at Ann Corlett's which the Blishes took, showing Charles feeding the donkey with a curiously publisher-like gesture ('. . . and there's more when you sign the contract . . .'); shots of the people who have helped me, Edmund Seagrave, Bruce Montgomery, Ted Carnell; Hilary, of course; and Hilary Moorcock; Kingers, of course, preferably at Trieste with Harry and the girls and me, jolly under sunshades and through drink at the Miramare beach; the kids playing tip-and-run on the lawn; the new electricity bill for fifteen pounds; the scratch pad by the phone; gum boots; the Volvo; the White Horse Hills, visible from my study window; Didcot Power Station, within an ace of being visible in the opposite direction; my sword; my Nebula award; Claude on the sward; milord abroad; the horde aboard; Maud, clawed, whored, adored; the Lord, awed; that 'ord' sound is one of the funniest in the English language—the Early Briton who invented it died laughing and they raised henges of stone over his grave; in long and in short, a book that might give some people some idea of a minute average life, and make them feel less alone; and in the back of every copy would be a disc you could play while leafing through it, which would shoot you the inimitable sound of traffic—mainly car-transporters, distinctively full or distinctively empty—kippling by on that toxic A420 between Oxford and Swindon, not a hundred yards away from the vulnerable areas of my cerebral vortex.

Perhaps Dick derived 'kipple' from Kipling? The verb form he uses is 'kipple-ized', but I seem to recall that back in the nineties, when the line of Aldiss had already disappeared in the mists of antiquity, J. K. Stephen used the name unadorned as a verb:

> When there stands a muzzled stripling
> Mute, beside a muzzled bore!
> When the Rudyards cease from Kipling
> And the Haggards Ride no more. . . .

Dick introduces his word through the mouth of J. K. Isidore, who lives alone in a great deserted apartment building, from which people have simply up and left: '. . . After that I just come home and go in my own place and I don't think about the rest. The apartments in which no one lives—hundreds of them and all full of the possessions people had, like family photographs and clothes. Those that died couldn't take anything and those who emigrated didn't want to. This building, except for my apartment, is completely kipple-ized. . . . Kipple is useless objects, like junk mail or match folders after you use the last match or gum wrappers or yesterday's homeopape. When nobody's around, kipple reproduces itself. For instance, if you go to bed leaving any kipple around your apartment, when you wake up next morning there's twice as much of it. It always gets more and more.'

This book should be kipple-ized with my kipple, bound in Lego, which is almost as much a part of my consciousness as of Clive's and Wendy's, end-papers full of children's kipple, that most love- and despair-producing kipple of all, with full-page full-colour plates of kids' dirty napkins and broken Matchbox cars and loved, neglected toys, and gallant plastic soldiers who have spent a weekend at attention in the flowerbed; and all the kipple I carry with me from house to house, right from long ago—the old copies of *Phoenix* (8 annas), with Windmill girl pin-ups and pictures of Lee Grant tanks advancing with 33 Corps towards the Irrawaddy; shot of the Space Needle in Seattle, signed by the Nourses; up to the piles of *T.L.S.* and *New Scientist* and *Theoria to Theory* and *Sight and Sound* that ravenously engulf my typescripts and correspondence shelves, if given a chance; and of course there's all the old correspondence itself, dating back to the early fifties, and all the old manuscripts in every stage; not to mention multiple volumes of diary containing millions of words written during the deserts of my first marriage, while I was unknowingly becoming a writer—and how ashamed of that invaluable repository of logorrhoea I am! I keep all that kipple in defiance of fame, knowing some day some institution—hardly likely to be in this country while the Leavises and Connollys are still kneeling round D. H. Lawrence—will make me a better offer than did Syracuse University (Syracuse offers nothing for author's kipple, I should explain, beyond a comfortable air-conditioned vault; but at least they welcome everything, from merest jottings to completed manuscripts, from tailors' bills to first editions, which suggests to my mind the proper and patient scholarly approach). We have boxes of stuff, all ready to be despatched to posterity! But first, some quick photographs for this book; sneak-previews of the books of mine that never got into print: my first novel, Dickens with a dash of Proust and Kafka for piquancy, *Shouting Down a Cliff*; *Twenty to Thirty*, written to find myself—and to a certain extent it worked but, ye gods, it must be an awful book; *The Hated Buckshee*, novel about the collapse of a marriage, written in despair, but perhaps not enough despair or enough something; notes for all the unwritten novels. The historical fantasy about the Nemanijas of Serbia is still on the cards; so, too, is *Life on the Textbook Level*; but will I ever get round to the ferocious *Man-Zoo* that I promised Fred Pohl? Fred, I did try!—If only your magazine looked more like a contemporary product, I would have been more encouraged. The battle must be to find next year's audience, not last (as you would personally agree . . .). There's a calendar on my wall from—yes, I swear it!—Scottish Aviation Limited; and the views of the Great Exhibition of 1851, the year Turner died; they'd be tipped in. Oh, it would be a splendid book!

We are a family who draw up our own treaties with kipple. As far as I know, my mother started it. She was always making Betty and me scrapbooks; I got the idea at an early age. Mother is gathering a new scrapbook for Timothy now. Betty covered a four-panel screen with kipple—and splendid it looks. Clive and I stud our holiday diaries with kipple. Wendy's dressing-table top is loaded with the stuff.

It's all an anagram of the mind, a way of not editing out your personality, a defence against tax and politics.

Faber's will never dare create the fabulous book I visualize. Create it yourself, readers! Obnubilate your minds with the friction of annual detritus! Tear out the pages of the book, shuffle, cut in extracts from old encyclopaedias, extra-illustrate, make the whole damned thing into a model of one minute's passing consciousness. Post it to me, if you can drag it as far as the post office; and we might get something as rich and varied as Chris Evans's cardboard boxes full of dreams.

Meanwhile, before I reach the end of my space and tether, there remain one or two important matters to attend to, matters emergent out of that good evening before the Soyuz space-station was built or two American teams put together the enzyme ribonuclease, three weeks back. I must come to the test and describe how I think the future might be better: which is to say, how people might live more happily and fruitfully in a couple of decades; which entails saying something about a way forward through the impasse at which our civilization has arrived.

To take that way forward, we shall need the aid of science. But is science, as it now lies within the hands of various bodies of various complexions, likely to aid such a far-out project as human happiness? Perhaps we can reach an answer by judging future achievements from past form.

And, to finish what I have begun in the Saviour's name, something must be said . . . the phone went: John Brunner this time, with his plans for enough activity this year, here and in America, to dismay any other two writers I know . . . about to move house, adopt (was it?) a Trinidadian mother and child, teach in the States, and with luck (as with me) collect a Nebula Award for his novel, *Stand on Zanzibar* . . . look, John, your kipple drives out mine; mine moves more slowly on a different level . . . so that the original sentence malforms on the page. See you in New York, hopefully! And Brazil certainly.

Oh yes, before discussing the possibility of a better future, something must be said about science fiction in the sixties, and *New Worlds*, and Chris Evans and me wondering the other night whether pumping money into the system might help, and deciding that it would not, not appreciably. Since sf will lead to the other issues, it shall come first.

14   A Cartographic Amis and Sixties SF

By the beginning of the 1960's, many rooms in the mansion of sf had been sealed off (though writers still work in those limbos, not realizing what has happened to them). They were sealed off by either bland popular acceptance—always a sign of a bluntened cutting edge in such forward sectors—or their self-appointed tasks as prophets being taken over by the new think-tanks, RAND, the Hudson Institute, and so on.

As strands of seaweed, home-made barometers, and weather-vanes—once standard equipment for amateur weather-forecasters —are now outdated and outclassed by orbital weather satellites, so the hit-or-miss fictional speculations of the Verne tribe are superseded by Herman Kahn and the bright guys of RAND.

(Serendipity. Another phone call. Charming Diane Lambert, *New Worlds'* publicity manager, asking if I would appear on a television programme with Moorcock and Ballard to chat about the future-in-the-present. I said okay, and we began talking about some of the people we wouldn't want on the programme, and from that to the subject of a friend of ours; perhaps he would not like his name mentioned, so let's call him Kit Monkhouse.

Kit began promisingly as a writer, made a small name through 'fanzines' (amateur magazines run by fans), published some science fiction, and has now graduated to writing horoscopes for a living. The horoscopes appear under a famous name and are obtainable only as free gifts, given away with Fangs, the Wonder Dog Food for Wonder Dogs.

Monkhouse wrote the Virgo horoscope. In order to obtain printed copies of his work, he is now touring London, buying up the tins of Fangs the Wonder Dog Food which sport the Virgo voucher. So much for prediction!)

Why do so many sf writers end by boosting Fangs or its equivalent? Or, to rephrase the question, why do so few make good as sf writers? Those who become known outside the field generally do so for reasons other than their science fiction. Fred Hoyle and Arthur Clarke would be sorry to live on their literary earnings alone, one imagines. The great exception is Ray Bradbury, a beautiful writer pole-axed by fame, whose sf gained general acceptance.

All sf writers in their starry-eyed, spotty-chinned phase desire either to save or destroy the world. Bearing this in mind, an sf writer who really made it is L. Ron Hubbard—a man who rocketed out of the pulps when he founded Dianetics (Scientology). Whether Hubbard is saving or destroying the world remains unclear; the untiring way in which authorities and reporters hound him suggests he has at least a dynamic mental equivalent of Fangs to sell. . . .

To look on sf as a sort of horoscopy is mistaken. Writers of sf who plead horoscopy as an excuse for their art deserve to have their work given away with dog food. Before RAND cropped up, horoscopy was perhaps a valid *post hoc* excuse for some readers reading some of the stuff, merely because nobody at all was in this sort of prediction business except the sf-writers. Now—nothing. But the horoscopy writers happened to set a trend: in the same way that the Life Insurance companies which became established in Victorian days slowly inculcated in the population the habit of thinking thriftily for the morrow.

The faster vehicles travel, the more necessary it is to see farther ahead; and our almost-captainless civilization is no different in that respect from a speeding stratojet. We must look as far ahead as we can. Sf can provide only faulty radar screens; nevertheless, it must be a matter of record that, while the literary establishment were scanning their Lawrence, Hemingway, Ivy Compton-Burnett, and other ikons, sf was demonstrating the need for such psychic radar screens—looking forward rather than back.

In a book published over here yesterday (*Digits and Dastards*), Fred Pohl has this to say in his introduction: 'There are three claims made for science fiction to prove that it is really something of great value: that it educates people to science, that it helps encourage young people to scientific careers, and that it predicts the technological advances of the future. What they say is true. No doubt about it. But there are science-fiction stories *and* science-fiction stories, and when they say those things about science fiction, they aren't talking about me.'

We have discussed the third item on Pohl's agenda. What of the other two? Does it help encourage young people to scientific careers? I know not of the States, and will take Fred's word for it. In England, the answer might also be in the affirmative: although if you really wanted to prove your case, you would have to show that this was not a case of *post ergo propter hoc*, and that the chaps weren't reading *Galaxy* because they had always had a scientific bent anyway.

What about sf educating people to science? Well, I suppose it does in a few cases; perhaps I have to stand forth as one item in

Fred's proof; but if it is so, there must be better ways of educating people. Most of science fiction is about as firmly based in science as eggs are filled with bacon. Most of them are based on older science fiction.

Fred, however, has magazines to run, and one may disagree with him here and there while appreciating that in his magazines he is bound to go forth crusading boldly. But, in a private introduction, he would have had at least one reader interested if he had gone on to say what he thought his stories *were* about. After John W. Campbell, Pohl is Second-in-Command of World Sf, and the view from his bridge could be enlightening.

From what he says, we can gather that there are other claims to be made for sf. I will make one now—an important one. Science fiction—the best contemporary science fiction, written not by rote but from conviction—is its own justification; and that is the definition of art.

With the arrival of the sixties, the state of the art was low, to judge purely from the magazines. Certainly, Ted Carnell, then editing *New Worlds*, ran a tolerable Dick serial, *Time Out of Joint*, but it was followed by a pretty fumbling Aldiss, *X for Exploitation* (also ill-famed as *The Interpreter* and *Bow Down to Null*). *Galaxy* ran Fred Pohl's *Drunkard's Walk*, which said nothing new, although it was set in a sort of TV university which had some novelty and interest. *F & SF* was running Robert Heinlein's *Starship Soldier* (later *Starship Trooper*), which I find, for ideological reasons, the least tolerable of all Heinleins. Only in *Astounding*, which I had by then almost ceased to read, was there sign of hearty life, in the serialization of Harrison's first big success, *Deathworld*. It exhibited the talent Harry has for keeping readers' eyeballs flattened to the page.

At that time, sf had yet to pick up new impetus. The great propaganda effort it had launched on behalf of space-travel was behind it, undigested. When the Sputniks went up in 1957—and by God, nobody predicted they would be *Russian!*—the circulation of sf magazines *dropped*. People wanted speculative writing, not *Practical Mechanics*.

I believe (and this one sentence may net me more angry mail than all the rest of the book) that it was the publication of Kingsley Amis's *New Maps of Hell* (London, 1961) which set the heavy ball rolling again. Amis took a certain critical position from which to examine the field; he dealt mainly with sf as an excellent vehicle for satire. *New Maps* is an enjoyable book still (that it is badly dated is partly a tribute to the effect the book has had); Kingsley was setting forth the best side of sf as it then was. His blind spot was that he did not enjoy the simple 'tale of wonder'; but at least he came out strongly against sf as a sort of prediction or popular education machine, and against the idea that one had to invent a special set of critical rules by which to judge it (a favourite fannish *bêtise* before the days of Anthony Boucher).

And he added this rider, which many found patronizing, but which still explains the attraction that newcomers to the field particularly enjoy: 'Often I think that part—and I mean part—of the attraction of sf lies in the fact that it provides a field which, while not actually repugnant to sense and decency, allows us to doff that mental and moral best behaviour with which we have to treat George Eliot and James and Faulkner, and frolick like badly-brought-up children among the mobile jelly-fishes and unstable atomic piles.'

Apart from his dig at the Establishment, Kingsley is making the point, I believe, that sf should not take itself too seriously. His quarrel with the sf scene at present would be—again this is my belief—that ever since his book, certain writers have taken themselves too seriously. To a large extent, he may be right; but one can't stay forever under the pier, playing with jelly-fish among the piles.

Undeniably, some writers have ruined themselves by trying to become 'serious'; I like several of them, and will mention no names. Sf, spec fic, or whatever you call it, is my life, and I'd be a fool not to take it seriously. But I also take seriously a further shade of meaning I read into Kingsley's remark; in the classical sense, any story set in the future becomes a comedy; it has removed itself from the possible (nobody is alive now in 1984); and, according to classical rules, comedy can only tell so much of life.

Which is not to say that comedy should not be taken entirely seriously. Leaving aside the unsuccessful *X for Exploitation*, of all my novels only *The Primal Urge* is no comedy; and that was intended as one. I have the impression, which may be totally misguided, that even in *Barefoot in the Head* I was writing black comedy.

To my mind, the vital history of sf in the sixties lies precisely in its taking itself more seriously: not as prediction: not as *Practical Mechanics*: not as private pabulum for those who loved Edgar Rice Burroughs as boys and have never outgrown him; not even as satire: but as science fiction. As one of the (minor) arts.

A word to amplify. Trad sf took all space and time as its stamping ground. 'Once upon a time, maybe two hundred million years ago, two galaxies were colliding.' A single story would be crammed with so-called 'ideas', which remained undeveloped, thrown in for kicks. Sometimes the big themes were there; but they were rarely treated with breadth of vision.

An exception is Isaac Asimov's *Foundation* trilogy, which covers a galaxy and ten thousand years; it has a grand theme, the survival of civilization against barbarism, and a grand idea, the idea of psycho-history. The loss is everyone's that the youthful Asimov's literary technique was not a match for his theme—indeed Tolstoi himself might have blenched and turned away. Asimov's habit of relating everything in brief scenes, without recourse to the superb art of narrative which, in the hands of accomplished writers, carries us nobly forward and gives especial emphasis to those selected moments at which the novelist allows us to be present, militates against his overall design; and so the telling denies the majesty of the subject. The one moment when sf might have become grand literature is lost. The creative impetus grows less steady; for the third Foundation volume merely echoes the jejune plot-mechanism of the second.

The lack lies not entirely with Asimov. He began writing at a time when the sf novel virtually did not exist in the sub-world of sf; there were only serial stories, a different kettle of fish; Asimov had to bow to the inattentive arbitration of magazine-readers. What he produced is good enough to inspire regret that he did not achieve the masterpiece we dimly see outlined in the air long after our rather pained re-reading has finished.

Grandiose concepts are fine; but execution must be finer. Science fiction is always fiction, even when it is not science.

Anthony Boucher saw this in the days when he was editing *F & SF*; but many of the stories he printed have technique and no creative impulse behind them—like many of the stories in *New Worlds*. At least interplanetary adventure is *about* something.

Sf is an entirety, like many other alloys. Britain's new decimal coins, the ten and five newpence-pieces, are cupro-nickel—neither copper nor nickel, but the two alloyed in specified amounts.

Sf is one of the rare alloys. Its content has to carry conviction, at least while we read; yet it is best if we are not convinced of the thesis before we begin (nothing more tedious than the musical that you visit already whistling its tunes).

Sf should be startling. Since we are more likely to be startled by probable events, it follows that sf on the whole functions best when set only a few years ahead. It's the stranger looming out of the fog two paces in front of you who makes you jump; fifty paces away, you dissipate the surprise element.

Be yourself—a worthwhile rule in life or literature and one that particularly interests me: for years, I didn't know who myself was to be!

Well, this is no textbook. These things seem simple enough. There are exceptions, and the rules of the game include this one: make each story an exception to the rules.

Only in this decade have rules and exceptions become more clear. Even the old die-hards no longer declare that you have to read everything before you can criticize anything. Just watch your step, that's all!

Most of this bursting-open process of sixties science fiction has been carried out by a small bunch of people. Before we start talking about that, I'm going downstairs for a drink and a look at Margaret and the moon.

15   New Worlds and SF Horizons of the Sixties

Wednesday, 29th January. Another bright mild night with the moon high. Insomnia can be caused by egotism; in my case, as often happens, I was thinking about what I was going to write next morning, unable to relinquish my thoughts, longing to get up and go back to work. Not a sound from Timothy; he never calls in the night. That luxuriant silence, when even the A420 is available to the fox, and the house makes its own noises. . . . I love the nights and their panoramas of silence as much as I used to hate them in childhood.

Many moons ago, cetiosaurs used to plod across this stretch of southern England. Their thin bugle-calls must have echoed over this very plot and their enormous matings thudded home where now the apple trees stand. What a swindle there aren't still a few about!

A plethora of mail this morning. People are out there somewhere, spindly successors to cetiosaurs. Particular bonus—a long letter from Mr. and Mrs. Barker on the history of Heath House. Mrs. Barker lived here for long periods before the 1939–45 war, under the régime of Mrs. Church-Wainright. She has strange and somewhat harsh tales to tell of those days. Thanks to the Barkers' kindness, we now have it all down on paper.

They also send photographs, of the house itself in various periods, and of its occupants. It has all been a little micro-climate of history. Again I'm full of the impulse to produce a monograph on it, including our fight to stop the planners putting a community centre on our field. Oxford University Press, perhaps?

But we were talking about sf in the sixties.

In 1960, I was living in two rooms on the ground floor of a house in Paradise Square owned by kind friends, George and Penny Halcrow—Penny being Edgar Wallace's daughter. In that year, *Non-Stop* made its first appearance as a Digit paperback. It had been a battle to find a publisher to accept it, despite the respectability of previous hardcovers. In that year too, I undertook the job of editing the first Penguin anthology, which appeared in 1961. Its immediate success surprised Penguin more than me; I knew sf was ready for a wide audience, and I could draw on the good work of the forties and fifties.

Penguin, however, thought there must be something 'in' sf, since John Wyndham's *Day of the Triffids* was still selling so fantastically ('as well as any Agatha Christie') after several years in print. John Christopher's *Death of Grass* was also bowling cheerfully along. Tony Godwin commissioned two more anthologies and later asked me to act as general editor of a new series of sf novels. From that task I had to resign when going to Jugoslavia in 1964, but by then several excellent titles had seen the light; among the novels for which I was responsible were Roy Lewis's *What We Did to Father*, which Richard Newnham at Penguin cleverly rechristened *The Evolution Man*; Blish's *Case of Conscience*; Russell's *Three to Conquer*; Herbert's *Dragon in the Sea*; Budry's *Who?*; and two for which I fought particularly hard, Ballard's *The Drowned World* and Clement's *Mission of Gravity*. Penguin paid the authors well; I believe I am correct in saying that nobody got less than £250 and one got £500. The sums were generous for those days, and set new standards of payment for sf in this country. The now-defunct paperback firm of Digit had paid me £75 for *Non-Stop*, not four years earlier.

A young man called Michael Moorcock used to come down to Oxford to talk to me in those days. He liked my stories and took the trouble to seek me out. I'd never met anyone like him—but then I'd never met anyone like anyone in those days. I lived within myself. Mike lived without. He assumed dandified airs, as much to amuse himself, I believe, as his girl friend, Sandra Hall, a lustrous sf fan. He was incredibly young, seventeen or something absurd, with a beautiful clear bare skin like a baby's bottom. Later, he became hairy overnight, and now somewhat resembles a Scarfe caricature of the French philosopher René Descartes.

It was because of Mike's support that I was elected President of the newly formed British Science Fiction Association. That was in 1960. In those days, I was obsessed with my separation from my children, Clive and Wendy; Mike was prepared to listen, and we traded troubles. We also discussed *Greybeard*, which grew partly out of my longing for the children and partly out of a splendid literary image Mike had of people travelling down a river.

In 1961, as President of the BSFA, I wrote to the author of *Lucky Jim* (as I then thought of him) and invited him to come to our Easter Convention as Guest of Honour. He came.

That was at Gloucester. Also present were Geoff Doherty, who had had his first sf anthology for schools published by John Murray, and a ball of American fire then living in Denmark called Harry Harrison. The convention was a roaring success. None of us stopped talking or drinking. ('You'll need your pep pills: nobody gets a wink of sleep': the fellow was right at last!)

Next year, I went over to stay with Harry and Joan and their two children, Tod and Moira, in Denmark, where they had come to rest after working northwards through Europe from Anacapri. Harry was still creating his fine and underrated novel, *Make Room! Make Room!*, and books on over-population and under-nourishment lay everywhere in his house. He was a fund of information about the scene in America: which of course was where it was all happening at that time.

My education continued the year after, in 1963, when Harry, Kingsley and I met again at the first International Festival of Science Fiction Films in Trieste as guests of honour. That was the funniest week of my life, I do believe. Harry and Kingsley (it's the sort of debt one does not mind being unable to repay) taught me to enjoy being a writer. That's a long while ago, but by God I *have* enjoyed it ever since!

After the festival, we slipped across the frontier, into the wilds of Istra, into Jugland. That magic word, 'Jugland', first registered on me shortly before the festival, when Kingsley was talking on the phone.

'We must be sure to take a look at Jugland,' he said.

'Where?'

'Jugland. Jugoslavia.'

We took a look. We all piled into Harry's Volkswagen and drove across the frontier in the mountains behind Trieste. The harsh beauty of the Istran peninsula overcame me. I determined to get back there as soon as I could.

Next year I was back—for six months. Margaret and I arrived in a snow blizzard and did not leave again till the peasants were tramping the first grapes. Our travels were eventually recorded in that one travel book to date, *Cities and Stones*.

Life had become somewhat kipple-ized in Jugland days. To escape paralysis, we bought an old second-hand Land-Rover which had already toured Turkey, and drove round the six republics of enchanted Jugland. It was what Dick terms 'rolling back the kipple-factor'. It really rolled then!

While we were travelling those dusty Jug roads, the last issue of Ted Carnell's *New Worlds* appeared: No. 141. The demise of *New Worlds* and its sister magazine, *Science Fantasy*, in which my first sf story had appeared, was already announced. No. 141 contained a reader's letter from Moorcock.

'As I have said elsewhere,' he wrote to Carnell, 'sf claims to be far-out when, in fact, it rarely is. It *should* be far-out—it needs editors who are willing to take a risk on a story and run it even though this may bring criticism on their heads. . . . You have discovered, encouraged and advised scores of young writers. It is probably due to your early encouragement that we nowadays have so many good writers in this country. . . . How, I wonder, is the potential to be found and trained in future?'

New Worlds did not die. Another company stepped in and bought it at the last moment. *New Worlds* and (*pro tem*) *Science Fantasy*, which became *Impulse* and then *Sf Impulse* during its last dying fling, were saved. One was to be edited by Moorcock himself (who brilliantly answered the question in his letter), the other by a friend of mine in Oxford, Kyril Bonfiglioli—another great conversationalist like Kingsley and Harry, but much more Regency in style. Those strange undertows of life were working again, for Bon had recently acquired, before he acquired *Science Fantasy*, Sanders and Co., the bookshop whose shutters I used to lob up and down when I first came to this city, Sanders and Co., the home of my Piranesis.

The intention was that Bon should take over *New Worlds*. As well versed in obscure Victorian and Edwardian science fiction as he was in paintings, books, or sabre-fighting, Bon loathed fantasy, or professed to do so. Mike, on the other hand, had been writing Elric fantasies for *Science Fantasy*, and so appeared to be the natural heir to that Carnellian throne. But there was a muddle: the barons signed the Magna Carta and King John went back to his royal caprices, in this version of history; Bon inherited *Science Fantasy*, while *New Worlds* 142 was edited by Michael Moorcock. Significantly, this issue carried the first part of a J. G. Ballard serial, *Equinox*, and an adulatory essay on William Burroughs by Ballard. It also contained a reader's letter from Ron Bennett, saying that the survival of the magazine had 'almost produced tangible happiness'.

In this time of tangible happiness, Harry and I, with the aid of Tom Boardman, were publishing our little magazine of professional sf criticism, *SF Horizons*. We were combative, as little magazines usually are, lavishing praise on very few writers, knocking the rest. James Blish secured us an interview with William

Burroughs, who revealed that C. S. Lewis was the writer to whom he felt closest; and I went over to Cambridge to record Kingsley Amis talking to C. S. Lewis.

We had great fun with our magazine, and great expense. Each issue cost us over £300, almost none of which we got back, since we had no distribution. Tom gallantly helped by compiling anthologies which covered costs, and Harry and I contributed free stories to the anthologies.

Such is serendipity—I've today received by post a bookseller's catalogue in which a copy of *SF Horizons* is offered for sale, mint, for one guinea. The bookseller is also offering some first editions of mine for eight guineas, which seems pretty cool!

We were cantankerous crusaders, Harry and I. Our second editorial begins, 'This magazine, the observant will have noticed, appears irregularly. It almost died between issues—by what must be regarded as coincidence, since science fiction itself almost died in the same period. Never has the field yielded such a yawn-provoking crop of reading matter . . .' etc. We were young then.

SF Horizons is now in deep-freeze, but its spirit remains volatile in the *Year's Best Sf* annual which Harry edits, and to which I contribute advice, complaints, and afterwords (and even stories, to the wrath of our rivals).

But to return to 1964, when I was driving through Jugoslavia and Mike was driving a stake through the heart of the old fiction. With his first *New Worlds*, a new epoch of sf began in this country.

By now, Mike's revolution is accomplished. Already, to many readers, all that happened before Mike's reign is forgotten. It should not be forgotten. Even the eerie headlights of J. G. Ballard had been glaring through the dark before that. It was Ted Carnell who published Jimmy's *Terminal Beach*, one of the most beautiful of all speculative stories.

And before that there had been other battles. Before the days of *New Worlds*, British writers had to make their fame and fortune abroad—i.e. in the States, a land that has always been generous and open-hearted to the British writer, no less in sf than in other sorts of writing. It is instructive to compare the careers of three earlier authors, each of whom, in youthful admiration, I once regarded as princes.

Eric Frank Russell started writing professionally in the late thirties. He aimed purely at the American market, and adapted his style accordingly. His camouflage was perfect, his mastery of American slang exact; and he never deviated from it. Now, it seems, he has ceased to write; at least, it is a long while since we had a new book, and the last few volumes to appear came from the bottom of his locker. In his heyday, he was one of the select band who made *Astounding* an event to look forward to. He made you laugh, too.

John Wyndham began earlier in the same way, writing for the Yankee pulps in the thirties, under his own name. Wyndham, an honest man and a modest one, would probably admit that those stories, although they met with success in their time, are unreadable now—to all but Sam Moskowitz, who was rash enough to reprint Wyndham's *Exiles on Asperus* of 1933 in his collection labelled *A Sense of Wonder* (*Three Stories* in the States).

After the war, taking a new name, Wyndham began again; using a plain English style, he caught a predominant mood with his disaster stories. Ballard has several times spoken derisively of Wyndham; yet Ballard's four novels to date have all been disaster stories—very different in tone, intent and effect, to be sure: but an evolution, not a revolution. Ballard is haunted not only by the deaths of American presidents but by the life of Wyndham.

Financially, *Day of the Triffids* must be the most successful sf novel of the last three decades.

Arthur Clarke arrived more recently than either Russell or Wyndham. He has fought and won his own battles, too. And bigger battles, at that. If the going is better for the rest of us as writers, much of this is due to Clarke. You don't have to enjoy his rather novelettish novels (though his *Childhood's End* is a serious and haunting work) or his clever and clean-limbed short stories to see why, for some people, he *is* British sf. For a time, he did seem to be all there was. He alone in the American magazines talked in an English tone of voice, his space heroes returned to London rather than New York, and chunks of cosmic culture got carted back to the British Museum rather than the Smithsonian. He helped, and still does, for his scientific interests lend muscle to his fiction just as George Stubbs's scientific interests do to his paintings. (Is Clarke also underrated like Stubbs—in the estimation of others, though not his own?)

True, there were rival native prodigies to Clarke in the early dawn light of the fifties: R. L. Fanthorpe (who was born, I suspect, within a stone's throw of me); E. C. Tubb; and the twin pillars of Scion Press, Vargo Statten and Volstead Gridban, both of whom were John Russell Fearn; but they were Grub Streeters, and none of their writings have established themselves—though Tubb's gritty and bleak stories of Mars, *Alien Dust* (1955), might well be worth resurrecting. Tubb also edited *Authentic Science Fiction* with some panache.

The lesson to be learnt from these excellent gentlemen of the pre-Moorcock era is two-fold; that while they all had to battle individually (as any writer must) and reach various levels of compromise which affected their quality, they also had to suffer collectively under the opprobrium of writing anything so odd as sf; and that although their battles somewhat aided their successors, readers of today have already forgotten about it. Just as I've forgotten about the twenties and the flourishing sf of the Edwardian era—because I never knew or cared.

Nor is it easy to write an impartial history of this little microcosm. The people involved are naturally not impartial, and husband their own prejudices. Critics outside the field like Kingsley are rare; good-hearted attempts to find out what is going on, like Patrick Moore's *Science and Fiction* (1957), get us nowhere.

Judy Merrill, Mike Moorcock and I once discussed writing a book between us, one third each, entitled: 'My Life in SF', but it sounded too silly. We were to do potted biographies of ourselves, since nobody else was fighting for the honour. Momentarily, we felt like Marlowe, Jonson and Shakespeare huddling together and saying, 'Think how grateful posterity will be!' So far, I seem to be the only one delivering, and that almost inadvertently. And I have gone far enough.

Briefly, since Moorcock took over, this country's sf has become lively as never before. Moorcock was the Prophet. Ballard was his Saint. When Judy Merrill arrived from America, she turned into Jehovah and pronounced the whole thing to be the New Wave. However the others involved in this spectacle have suffered by it. Moorcock himself has certainly emerged charged with potential.

It could be said that the gospel spread to the States. But the most interesting new writers (those who cared greatly for subject and form as well as style) lived in London at one time or another: the quirky Thomas Disch, John Sladek and Pamela Zoline. Good British writers have also sprung up, like David Masson, Langdon Jones and possibly Charles Platt; none of them are prolific, but then that's part of the reform: that you don't have to burst out with novelettes all over to make your mark. The *réclame* of la Zoline and Masson rested for a long while on one story apiece.

Nor must it be forgotten that the fresher breezes have attracted poets, such as D. M. Thomas, George Macbeth, Bill Butler and Peter Redgrove. (Robert Conquest, another poet, who also wrote a sf novel, is of an earlier generation.) And, with the poets, artists and designers, men like Richard Hamilton and Paolozzi, whose work has appeared in reproduction in *New Worlds* and stimulated writers as well as readers. This great mixing together of different disciplines achieved its testimony at the 1968 two-day Conference in Brighton on 'Science Fiction and its Influence on Other Arts', chaired by Professor Asa Briggs and Edward Lucie-Smith.

In the States, for reasons perhaps not unconnected with pervasive doubts concerning the space race, new movements similar to the one in England are slow to take place. There are some promising newcomers working, such as Barry Malzberg and Norman Spinrad, the author of *Bug Jack Barron*—and of course those who have contributed to the lifeblood of *New Worlds*: Sladek, Sallis, Delaney, Disch, Zoline, Harvey Jacobs, Harlan Ellison and Roger Zelazny. Zelazny has had to battle against fannish adulation; he looks like being successful, although for a while his style became increasingly rococo, to no good effect. But fans love rococo.

In England, fandom is less dangerous. The American fans are great adulators; over here, the prevalent note is the whine of miniature critics. Mercifully, there are exceptions on both sides of the Atlantic, as well as a brisk interchange of influences—which always, until possibly the last few years, has benefitted Britain.

Meanwhile, mainstream sf continues to rely heavily on adventure material with tin men, a lot of thuggery, not a little sword-and-sorcery, and disneyland astronomical effects—two pink moons and a blue sun rising in the west. Writers like William Tenn, Cyril Kornbluth, Frederik Pohl, Phil Dick, Phil Farmer, Robert Sheckley, Kurt Vonnegut, and many others (not to mention critics like Damon Knight) begot new subjects out of thin air and dazzled us all. The dazzle should soon be starting again. The world is full of new subjects, once one forgets about Flash Gordon.

Dark is coming down again at Heath House. Metallic things glitter and flit behind our barricade of trees. As Browne said on a marginally similar occasion, with perhaps a passing reference to my *Hothouse*: 'But the Quincunx of Heaven runs low, and 'tis time to close the five ports of knowledge: We are unwilling to spin out our awaking thoughts into the phantasmes of sleep, which often continueth praecognitions: making Cables of Cobwebbes and Wildernesses of handsome Groves.'

16   *Automation versus Fact-Free Education*

Thursday, 30th January. 'How's the book going?' Margaret asks.

'I hope it's more a gallimaufry than a hodge-podge!'

'Gallimaufry certainly sounds better. . . .'

I climb into my bath.

'Locked in that Delphic ambiguity which torments our daily lives. . . .' Loren Eiseley, in his introduction to David Lindsay's *Voyage to Arcturus* which Ballantine have sent me. 'The Delphic ambiguity which torments. . . .' Yes, that's what Dick and Ballard and A. E. van Vogt manage to convey.

We are booked to go and see Albee's play, *A Delicate Balance*, with Peggy Ashcroft, next Monday at the Aldwych. Splendid! Hilary almost insisted we should go.

Letter from Clive. He never misses. From birth, he has been a unique person. Also a rare letter from Wendy, in form of a newspaper: WENDY'S OWN. Your Paper. 6d.

Headlines: WENDY STARTS TO PLAY THE FLUTE. WANTED TO CHANGE BUT DOES NOT KNOW

WENDY HAS PIANO LESSONS EVERY FORTNIGHT

WENDY ON 3rd CHAPTER OF HER BOOK

WENDY ILL 16th JANUARY. FELL OFF PONY INTO FLOODED
DITCH—HURT BACK AND LEG

The sheet includes 'personal letter to all at Heath House', good
wishes from the editor, and fashion hints. Also love from WENDY'S
OWN.

The girl most likely to succeed!

There is a postal strike in London, so here endeth my mail.

So I ask the final utopian question: how could we manage that
people like Clive and Wendy and Timothy and their children and
children's children will live more happily and fruitfully? Is it
possible to match the immense proliferation of technology and
automation with an extension here and there of rational thought?
So that more genuine freedoms than we enjoy will exist in future?

Take this postal strike, for instance. The wrangle is ostensibly
about the usual things, shorter hours, better pay and productivity.
What are its underlying reasons? One reason that occurs readily
lies buried in pre-history: that man is a hunter rather than a farmer
(there's a splendid fantasia on this subject in Nigel Calder's *The
Environment Game*), and cannot take to the monotony of diurnal
routine. As Priestley said, it's not natural to work from nine till
five every day. For post office workers, the seasons are marked
officially only by the increased volume of work at Christmas. You
would expect these men, if they were striking for the reasons
stated by unions and politicians, to dislike the increased Christmas
work. They don't. Anyone who has worked in sorting offices and
elsewhere over the Christmas season knows that the atmosphere
is especially cheerful then. New faces are about, there is a change
of pace. The imposed routine is broken. Routine, monotony;
there's the enemy.

The oppressive early days of the Industrial Revolution are
comparatively far behind us, and with them such ills as child
labour, cancer of the scrotum (common to chimneysweeps) and
almost endemic tuberculosis. But we have still to devise a way to
banish the spirit-break of boredom. The routines upon which our
consumer system depends do not allow full recognition of the
great annual roll of seasons, never mind the lesser swings of a
man's own axial variations.

The mechanistic tendency is always towards annihilating
seasons, towards the constantly lit broilerhouse, towards the farm

as a monoculture and the individual as a unit. Uniformity is machine-utopia.

Air-conditioned cities are already on the agenda. Who will get their dome first—L.A., New York, Kuwait, Irkutsk, or a yet unbuilt city on the Moon? Under that dome, new monotony-ratings will be achieved.

Wherever the domes go up, there will be riots. Man has his seasons. He is a walking biosphere. In his glands, in his old brain, as well as in his expectations, he has his circadian rhythms. His dilemma is that he cannot dispense with his machines or tolerate the monotony they engender.

One escape-route from oppressive routine has been aired in science fiction. Free men from work and put in their places creatures that do not suffer from monotony: robots, machine men, androids. Automation is now proceeding (though noticeably less rapidly than was predicted when the word 'automation' came into general use after World War II, thanks to the inertia of society and general misoneism). But the idea of freeing men needs examination.

Freeing them for what? Men whose unions gain them a shorter working week merely work the old hours and earn more pay. They want not freedom but cash. 'Moonlighting' has meant various ills: once it was the committing of what Chambers's dictionary calls 'agrarian outrages' in Ireland by night, about 1880; before that, in England, it meant moving house by night to evade land-lords; now, in the States, it means multiple job-holding: a job by day, a job by night. There is a general rejection of leisure. We are not yet ready for total freedom. Compulsory freedom tomorrow would mean a wave of suicides the day after.

Understandably. Fish of the shallow seas are lost in the great deeps beyond the continental shelf. One has to be educated to leisure as to everything. Freedom from work is not enough by itself. I should be unemployed if I was not a writer. One must be employed. Nigel Calder holds hunting to be the great activity: everyone should hunt—with camera rather than gun.

Nobody has ever decided what men could do if they did not work or hunt. The monotony of non-work is every bit as lethal as the monotony of routine-work. With high populations, the problem becomes far more intractable. (In Bob Silverberg's *The*

Time-Hoppers, the unemployed proles of Eastern Seaboard go in
for lotteries and mechanical games: debased forms of hunting.)

There is a world of difference between enjoying leisure and
having leisure thrust upon one. The go-getting nations of Wesciv
fear leisure at present: it implies Be Not Do. Re-education is
necessary. Nor need such an aim be utopian. With mass-communication we have the means, and with the slow advance of
automation the time, to educate for leisure.

The problem is not insoluble. If it seems so this is partly
because we fail to visualize what will follow automation—and so
we imagine a vacuum. We see all the factories and offices emptied
of men, and wonder where they can all go, what they can do. In
fact, the process is a slow one—disappointingly slow—and during
it other occupations are emerging, some of which we can only
guess at as yet.

We can understand by analogy how complete revolutions like
automation effect people's ways of life. One of the best analogies
is the change-over from stage-coaches to railways, a very abrupt
change which occurred in the late 1830's and 1840's (the opening
of Brunel's Great Western Railway between Paddington and
Bristol in 1841 put an end to the glorious Bristol coach): one of
the great decisive periods in western history, when the ethos of an
industrial state 'took', in a way in which it has still not properly
taken in, say, India, despite many years of trying.

Outside London, in the 1830's, Hounslow was a considerable
coaching centre. It was situated at the junction of the Exeter, Bath
and Gloucester routes; no less than 170 mail and stage coaches
rattled through Hounslow every day. The great Billy Chaplin
alone had 150 horses there, and all told there were about 2,500
coach and posting horses. Barnet, on the Great North Road,
boasted about 800 coach horses. In less than a decade, all was gone.

In 1830, England had 97 miles of railway track; in 1840, 1,497
miles. In 1845, Parliament authorized 4,800 miles of track to be
laid that year. What happened to the people involved?

Billy Chaplin did not worry—he became chairman of the railway company that drove his coaches off the road. This is how
Leslie Gardiner describes what other people did, in his book,
Stage-coach to John O'Groats: 'Some were going into cartage for
the railways and breweries; the Patersons and Pickfords, the

Barclays and Tennants were already making new names in new fields. Some had become undertakers, some even station-masters. Everywhere, the four-in-hand business was running down, with fewer and fewer coaches on the road—and those dirty and patched-up—with more and more clumsy and inexperienced youths handling them; for the swell dragsmen were buying country inns as fast they could, or marrying landladies, or going on to the city omnibuses, or quietly drinking themselves to death.' A lot of the great coaching yards were turned into railway sidings. Their staffs found jobs in the new towns.

Automation is not as sudden or as dramatic as this. But it will bring—is bringing—new ways of thought. Fear of, or indeed resistance to, those new ways of thought is useless; they will rise as surely as the tide. Nor can they be any less drastic than the new ways of thought which accompanied the railways.

Because those new ways are now old, they bear re-examining.

It was the speed of the railway which most impressed the early Victorians. Could a man really travel at twenty-five miles per hour and not have his neck dislocated?

Just as fundamental as speed was the fact that the railways, despite their tiresome divisions into classes of carriages, were democratic. To travel by rail cost very much less than coaching, as well as being safer and more comfortable. For the first time, it was possible for something more than a minute fraction of the population to move about their own country. The six million people who visited the Great Exhibition in 1851 would scarcely have contemplated doing so two decades before, when the great coachroads were hardly fit to travel by foot for half the year. The railways opened the country for a new democracy.

Not only passengers became mobile. Freight took on new concepts. The railways did superbly what the canals had laboured cumbrously to do at the turn of the century. Almost anything could be transported anywhere, without weeks lost in transit. From this new mobility arose Britain's industrial supremacy.

Even people's ideas of time were altered. Railways work to more rigid timetables than stage-coaches. Time was no longer the hour that corresponded with the parson's turnip or the village clock; time was firmly in the custody of the metropolis.

The processes of regularization so markedly reinforced in Europe in the fourteenth and fifteenth centuries, when town clocks were beginning to induce regularity within cities (a petition presented to the town council of Lyon in 1481 emphasizes the need for 'a great clock whose strokes could be heard by all citizens in all parts of the town. If such a clock were to be made, more merchants would come to the fairs, the citizens would be consoled, cheerful and happy and would *live a more orderly life*, and the town would gain in decoration')—these regularizing forces took another great stride forward with the railway system.

'Everything is near, everything is immediate,' cried Sydney Smith in 1842. It is not impossible for us to empathize with the overwhelming feeling of change, of defiance of the natural order, which seized men and women at that time: such men as Darwin, born in 1809; Thackeray, born 1811; and Dickens, born 1812. The thousands of miles of railway line, with all they entailed and presaged, cut that generation off for ever from the apparently unaltering world of their childhood.

Thackeray catches the whole matter in one sentence in his essay *De Juventute*: 'We who lived before railways, and survive out of the ancient world, are like Father Noah and his family out of the Ark.'

Every generation since has complained of change, with less good reason than Thackeray. In the 1960's, whiskers on youthful faces, pop music, LSD and heart-transplants have provoked more idle nonsense from an ageing generation than all the miles of railway ever did (it's easier to be vocal, audibly, nowadays).

It's high time people got used to change, and to the idea that one constant and reliable thing is change. The human condition doesn't grow worse, and people don't grow more degenerate, any more than they grow better. The oldest sliver of mouldy papyrus dug up in Babylon contains the thrilling message, when deciphered, 'Things aren't what they used to be.'

In the golden days when everyone wears my wards on their wrists, boys, then we'll be free of facts, and education can work on things like accustoming us to the idea of change: to the idea that society, by its nature, is always pressing on, even if we have no notion of the ultimate goal.

Automation can then be seen as one of the still-spreading effects caused when the first navvy dug the first spade of earth to build the first mile of railroad track. (And no doubt he was grumbling because he had lost his old job on the canals!)

Let us suppose, then, that this country solves its union troubles (the part-cause of this postal strike, as of many others) and enters an era of full automation, so that many more people can enjoy much more leisure. Then education can come into its own.

Education is not a negative thing, a mere antidote to ignorance. Get it away from the inky stigma of the schoolroom, and it can be recognized as a way of life. Basically, it partakes of both the hunting and farming way of life; it is both a hunt and a form of cultivation; while increasing knowledge and experience compensate both hunter and farmer for stiffening muscles.

So the new leisure-patterns can be filled by fact-free education. Education can take over show business, just as the opposite sometimes appears to be happening now. It can promote special topics to interest the old; and the old can participate in special projects to help the young. The human race is one, and not a bundle of conflicting age-groups, as consumer interests would have us believe.

We are slowly learning that sex is not something that stops in middle age. Like the lettering in seaside rock, even when faint and distorted, it goes right through life. What I have called for convenience fact-free education (we will examine the idea more closely in a short while) can also go on through life, nourishing life. We know almost nothing about ourselves; it would be a genuinely enriching process for us to learn more—provided we were an active and contributing part of that process: more teaching than taught against!

17   Christie and the New Fantasy-Dramas

Another direction towards which fact-free education must work is in improving our understanding of the relationship between crime and punishment. The strike of the postal workers could be stopped by repressive measures; most extremely, a law could be passed whereby the act of going on strike was categorized as sabotage against the state, punishable by death. Many people throughout the country would support this. 'They ought to shoot the bloody lot!' you hear people say, when dockers walk out or car factories close.

However, it is generally agreed by more enlightened persons that such methods are not only atavistic but impracticable. A better idea is to find the cause of the discontent which leads to strikes and cure that. Some such steps certainly have been taken, within the rough-and-tumble between managements and men of our capitalist society, but they still have to go a long way to remove basic grievances.

In a public case like a big withdrawal of labour, we do vaguely see that punishment—of men or managements—is no solution, however many million man-hours the nation loses yearly through strikes. In other realms, even where it may be just as inappropriate, punishment is evoked instinctually. And instinctually is the right word. The old animal brain is at work, striking out at whatever offends, and then forgetting what it did.

This response is seen at its crudest in the system of capital punishment. A multiple murderer, even such an odious specimen of the breed as John Reginald Halliday Christie, the necrophile who was hanged in 1953 after making away with possibly a dozen women, has valuable lessons for the community. Once he is caught, he cannot harm the community; but the community insists on revenge. Yet the act of murder is most often itself an act of revenge. So the chain of violence is perpetuated.

Odious though Christie was, he should also be the subject of pity. Screwing dead girls may not be socially acceptable, but it could be understood as Christie's pathetic attempt at normality. His father was all we mean by 'a strict Victorian', a martinet with a violent temper, unapproachable, uncommunicative, who believed in hard wretched walks on Sundays and good thrashings to teach the boy to be manly. By way of compensation, his mother spoilt and fussed him; he was her 'favourite'. His genetic make-up was such that, between his two parents, Reggie couldn't manage to grow up to get what we all want, and deserve to get, in any socially acceptable way.

Operatively, Reggie's father is still alive, multiplied by thousands, striking out against individuality and sexual pleasure. And this sort of petty aggression breeds many other types of aggression (one type: some postal workers may be motivated in part by the desire to defy the father-figure of the G.P.O.). Reggie's father, we can be sure, would be all for capital punishment; and he too was once a vulnerable child . . . and so back to Cain.

Such repressed individuals find relief in vicarious violence, of which capital punishment is one example. The BBC and the newspapers acknowledged the prevalence of such repression-needs when they described a recent large-scale demonstration by London students in Grosvenor Square, which was carried through without violence, as 'a failure'; it was a failure only from the point of view of those who were hoping a few heads would be bashed in.

Such people do not always relish violence when it comes home to them: war is not necessarily to their personal taste. But they may influence public opinion towards war, in their excitement at the smell of violence before the war begins. During the Cuba missile crisis, or at similar times when cool heads are needed, such pressure on politicians could be decisive, and tip the already delicate balance between war and peace.

The role mass media play in cultivating an atmosphere of violence is considerable; it has been estimated that the American child sees some thirteen thousand deaths-by-violence on TV between the age of five and fourteen. What effect this has is open to debate: but less open than what effect similar viewing has on mature adults; we can at least agree that the tendency is not good. At the very least, the idea is conveyed that one token of manliness is to sock people on the jaw, if not to shoot them dead. *Violence in mass media does nothing to counteract violence in real life.* Those of us who have children know that learning is achieved by imitation.

Boredom is one of the fertile fields in which violence and war can grow. As a lad before World War II, I was subject to boredom, the boredom that comes from lack of direction. The war was exciting; evil was loose in the world. Many of my elders found that war solved, or at least shelved, their personal problems. Partly this was because in wartime there is greater sexual laxity. Men and women in their forties and fifties or older find fresh chances to be in love and make love. During the Blitz on London, suicide rates significantly dropped, psychiatrists found themselves for the first time without clients.

These are problems of aggression and frustration that education at present comes nowhere near tackling; they form no part of any curriculum. Yet my dictionary defines education as 'strengthening of the powers of body or mind'.

Our present educational system has grown from fact-stuffing curricula. When the system of wards, by which one can have any known fact at one's fingertips, comes in, education can then begin properly to strengthen the powers of body and mind. It must begin to teach non-violence, and try to liberate us from all the repressive forces that distort us as individuals-in-society.

Whether this can be done, nobody knows. Mainly because it has never been tried.

What I picture, naïvely I admit, is a series of fantasies: dramas that have their roots in present group-therapy sessions. Role-playing, that essential which enables us to find some sort of place in life, will be encouraged. For is not role-playing one of the reasons why we now surround ourselves with fantasy, with pro-liferating media which offer us chances of different shadow-lives, of identifying with other people more evil, more successful, or more saintly, than ourselves? And isn't this need for fantasy a sign of how insecure we are in a changing society? If we could be sure of the chance, early in life, to be sure of ourselves later in life, many of today's miseries would be things of the past. Fact-free education might be the death of literacy; it could be the birth of real civiliza-tion.

This is a time of crisis (as many times have been, but now we glimpse chances for ultimate failure or ultimate success), when some such radical attempt to solve that 'Delphic ambiguity which haunts our daily lives' is pressingly necessary. The war's being waged in the brain—between, to put it anatomically, the neocortex and limbic brain; or between, as Arnold Toynbee puts it, in a more old-fashioned metaphor, the head and the heart.

In his wise book, *Change and Habit: The Challenge of Our Time*, Toynbee says this: 'The misfit between head and heart is bound to cause trouble because the human psyche—fractured though it is into a conscious and subconscious component—must nevertheless act as a unity if it is to have any chance of controlling the situations in which it finds itself or into which it brings itself. This unity in action is necessary because either of the two components has it in its power to frustrate the other—and thereby to incapacitate the psyche as a whole—if the other component tries to act independently, without regard for its yoke-fellow. . . . In the head's intellectual realm of science and technology, the head can race forward at a speed that the heart cannot emulate. Consequently the head is constantly taking the heart by surprise by confronting it with revolutionary new situations. . . .'

Toynbee's is another way of approaching the problem that concerns Koestler—that concerns everyone. More than ever, we need to become whole.

The moving band of technology, that conveyor belt on which we are all carried, may present us in the near future with a revolutionary new situation where we could allow the psyche the chance to become whole. I refer to the situation when (and if—but we will discuss the 'if' presently) we in the western world get the chance of what I have called 'fact-free education', the education that will attend to hearts as well as heads.

This is how I visualize this revolutionary new system coming to pass.

More sophisticated computerization, computer languages that differ diminishingly less from spoken English, quantal improvement of communications, integration of media, modernization of present knowledge-repositories, international linkages of information-stores, microminiaturization of all hardware, with consequent speeding and proliferation of the artifacts concerned, reinforced software facilities: these things are on the way and can be read on extrapolative graphs converging to a point—let's say, for argument's sake, in the 1990's—where fact-free education as I outline it becomes possible: whole areas of thought-systems and fact-correlatives will be available to everyone in the same way that light and power are now available. (And the hunger for facts is there, just like the hunger for fuel power: after the Bible and Spock, *The Guinness Book of Records* is Britain's best-seller!) As the railways brought a newer, truer democracy, so will this on-coming revolution.

This is why the work of people like Evans and many others is of importance. A deadline is set. We have to understand more about the brain, and about the subtle interactions between head and heart. We have to understand so that life-education can be set up, in the 1990's or whenever. The whole thing will not come about overnight (of course it may never come about); but it may come about as dramatically as the turnover from coach to rail.

There are encouraging signs that many people are ready for just such a revolutionary move. The general disillusion with politics; the impatience of the younger generation with worn-out systems of education and government; the distaste for self-perpetuating institutions; the cool familiarity of a generation still at school with a wide variety of psyche-touching problems, such as war, sex of all inclinations, and drugs; a growing indifference towards the 'bigger means better' attitude of technical demagogues; and the excellent furore of the arts. Under wise leadership, all such movements could be channelled into a revolution of heart.

How the fantasy-dramas will work, I don't know. I'll tell you in twenty years. But clearly we have a good guide to the sort of things they will involve: the symbolism of dreams with which we are nightly involved. We want a drama more crazy, more logical, than the paintings of de Chirico or Dali or Richard Hamilton, or whoever you care to mention, more deep-biting than any of our modern plays, more liberating than any novel or poem.

Education will then start being fun—something you can't stay away from. Head-learning will still continue, of course, for the automated world will offer new skills and careers; this more traditional side of education will also catch fire from the new experiments. As for the heart-learning, mime, dance, straight acting: all will be grist.

The whole world of youth will be a stage and all the boys and girls in it players; and each one in his time will play many parts. The audience will be the older generation (many stricken dumb or garrulous with dismay), the talent-spotters the equivalent of present-day teachers. They will see which of the many parts best suits each player, and will judge and guide accordingly, if the players cannot themselves decide. Thus the weak will be succoured and given what help may be needed; the little Reggie Christies will be given suitable compensation for repressive fathers.

Nor will older generations be mere onlookers. They will have their turn too as the whole movement develops. In the widest sense, education is a lifelong thirst, and seems capable of satisfying heart and head. We can learn from what we do correctly, as well as from our mistakes, and perfection as well as failure needs its proper platform. There will be more leisure in a fully automated age; very well, here is one of the new things that will fill it: fantasy-dramas. Hollywood, Shaftesbury Avenue, Broadway, can merge with Eton, Princeton, and the Tavistock Clinic. We need a new art-form to express total man.

Oh yes, it's an almost impossible idea. So are all untried ideas. Space travel was 'twaddle' in 1956. Within fourteen years, men were walking about on the moon. Within twenty years, people could be walking about on earth, at peace with themselves. There are plenty of people already perfectly good at that sort of counselling role; I've come across them in doctors' surgeries and in Marriage Guidance clinics. They're everywhere: people who would love to be engaged in fruitful schemes to help others.

The first generation will be most difficult. After that, the new ideas will have penetrated the homes in which future babies are born. Children will soon adapt—and they will discover in the fantasy-dramas whole families of life-enhancing properties.

But could we do without aggression and violence? Are they not valuable? Isn't aggression an essential ingredient, an inheritance from our distant animal past, and from man-the-hunter's past?

We don't know how essential aggression is until we try for the first time to control it on a major scale. Our animal past needn't worry us here, for Man is the only species that indulges in intra-species warfare. Animals don't kill their own kind; as Lorenz has shown, even wolves have their formulae for avoiding violence. Our animal past is on the side of non-violence.

Mankind is still evolving; that evolution needs a helping hand; everyone agrees in their neocortex that war is bad. Right, let's help stamp it out where it begins: in the home—in our own homes as well as Christie's home.

Perhaps to encourage us in this uphill task, we might consider a word I have already used once or twice: non-violence.

Non-violence is a very old idea. Jesus had a few words to say on the subject. In our century, it has acquired new force. Among the ghastly proliferation of types of warfare stands this flower non-violence struggling with the weeds.

Not pacifism: non-violence. Gandhi used non-violent methods and, with favouring circumstances, it got the British out of India; the British withdrawal may seem inevitable now, but in 1939 it was as unimaginable to the average man as space travel.

Martin Luther King also showed that non-violent methods worked: and against opponents with highly superior destructive power.

No book is an island; each book rests on a library. I quote from my library whenever possible. Jerome D. Frank's volume on *Sanity and Survival* (1968) has some highly relevant reflections on non-violence. He points out that non-violent action is not a single technique but a new class of fighting, in which strategy and tactics differ from campaign to campaign.

'The second great achievement of Gandhi and King is that in two different societies and with people whose traditions are very different, *they have reversed the relationship between masculinity and violence,* and shown that this may be based more on cultural expectations than on the usually assumed biology of maleness.' (My italics.)

Could this really be so? It's pretty good, isn't it? One piece of evidence Frank brings to support this wild notion is the experience of Negro children who persisted in a lunch-counter sit-in in Oklahoma City. All stressed their persistent feeling of latent power during the sit-in, derived from the strong conscious sense of being able to control their own aggressive feelings in the service of ideals.

Other people who participated in similar demonstrations spoke of a heightened sense of manliness and a feeling of moral superiority over opponents—who, in effect, act out their own aggressive feelings for them.

I repeat the biological evidence for the success of non-violence: we have a long animal inheritance behind us, and it is the human in man who attacks his fellow men, not the non-aggressive animal. In this respect, even the wolves are shining guiding lights to man.

While I've been writing this book, non-violence has spread into a new campaign; or rather, the self-immolation of Jan Palach in Prague gives fresh and poignant identity to the Czechs' non-violent struggle against the repressive forces of Soviet Communism.

Non-violence can't always win. Nothing always wins. But perhaps it can sometimes win where no other method would succeed. As, we hope, in Czechoslovakia, eventually.

Non-violence certainly works on the individual level. So does the allied virtue, lenience. Of course, it's no good being lenient from a position of weakness: people spot that a mile off and laugh. But to be lenient from a position of power can be (not invariably because there are few invariables in human behaviour) staggeringly successful. To be lenient and forgiving when one could strike out or say something wounding is as impressive now as ever it was. What's more, it generally impresses both sides.

Lenience is an effective deterrent, perhaps as much with children as with adults. Again, Frank reports an experiment in which children were dissuaded from playing with an attractive toy; some were threatened with harsh punishment, some with mild punishment. Later, they were asked to rate the attractiveness of the toy. Those threatened with severe punishment still found it attractive; those threatened with mild punishment 'derogated it', as Frank says. The idea is 'that the child must be able to explain to himself why he behaves inconsistently by avoiding the attractive toy. The threat of severe punishment for playing with it is sufficient reason, so he can still regard it as attractive; but if the threatened punishment is too mild to justify his avoidance, the most readily available reason is that the toy wasn't attractive after all'.

In other words, if you want to change someone's attitude, you threaten them just enough to get compliance yet not enough to provide inadequate justification for that compliance. Try it next time small boys steal your apples.

Such ideas need more testing out. But they could be useful in fact-free education. (The economist, Kenneth Boulding, has invented a law: What exists is possible. So my fact-free education exists.) I would like to see a new generation of teachers starting with the idea that lenience and non-violence promote manliness, and see if that doesn't make for more happiness all round than the current preoccupations with violence.

Today's younger generation is full of ideas and assurance (most generations are!), and anxious to assist in its own teaching. Such drives would be canalized in fact-free education. Only when the system was established might people realize how much aggression is merely frustrated creativity—or, at the least, frustrated expectations.

Friday, 31st January. While I was gainfully employed up here last evening, talking about improved communications, the TV news was covering the postal strike. Margaret told me about it when I went down to watch the first part of Dostoevsky's *The Possessed*.

'The mail's piling up. . . . The Postmaster General has stopped the fourpenny post rate, just like that!'

'Stopped the fourpenny post! By gum, lass, country's gooing to t'dogs!'

'Ay, and who knows where t'dogs is gooing!'

To relieve the boredom brought on by people like the Postmaster General, we slump into mock-Yorkshire, mock-Scottish, mock-Norfolk, mock-Oxon, and mock-Macmillan voices. We also have our own peculiar language. When Timothy utters his favourite cries, something between niggling and real howling, he is said to be 'heegling'. The act of love-making, when carried out with a certain jovial animality, is 'creaturing'.

Margaret Kent, my new secretary, comes this morning. Very hopeful. Telephone bill arrived this morning—that got through the postal *cordon sanitaire* safely! Our phone has been working overtime. Philip Strick of the British Film Institute, arranging our session at the National Film Theatre in March; the Camden Hurst Hotel down in Milford-on-Sea, arranging for us to stay there with Clive and Wendy at half-term, in a fortnight; Amis; Ballard; Platt; Guy; Boardman; even Ted Carnell; the fine weather is bringing people out of hiding. Mama moves into her new home next month; in March, the new baby is born; then off to Rio de Janeiro for the film festival; in April, the convention; in May, Harry arrives. . . . It's going to be a busy year—and a short one, with our excursion to California in December.

Not only will the fantasy-dramas of fact-free education be fluid and symbolic, based on the tutelary genius of dreams; dreams themselves will be used, discussed, made working tools for strengthening the well and the weak. That dreams can foreshadow psychosis is well known (R. D. Laing gives some examples in his *The Divided Self*, where pre-psychotic dreamers were engulfed in fire, or the petrifaction of others occurred).

The result of all this submergence in fantasy will be, paradoxically, a freedom from fantasy in adult life: for adult life will run with less conflict with itself and with less conflict with the outside; hence, there will be less of the present need to escape from self.

For there to be less conflict between man and his work, careers will have to be reshaped. Work will have to fit man, rather than the present case of man having to fit work. That is a large subject; but why should work not fit man? In our contemporary world, it cannot fit, for multitudes of people cling to boring jobs they despise for fear of striking out into something more interesting (I know the hearts of booksellers' assistants); they are at odds with themselves and society, and society is so corrupt that at best only an uneasy truce can be made with it.

Even with nothing else changed, plenty of humdrum jobs could be made very much more enjoyable (booksellers' assistants should not be forbidden to read the books they are there to sell).

When should this fact-free education start? My answer would be—from the cradle. In his story *I Always Do What Teddy Says*, Harry Harrison presents a small robotized Teddy which can talk. 'Teddies have the vocabulary and outlook of the very young because their job must be done during the formative years. Teddies teach diction and life history and morals and group adjustment and vocabulary and grammar and all the other things that enable men to live together as social animals.' Harry's Teddy is going to be very useful. It is, in fact, the form that wards will take in my posited future before a child is old enough to enjoy the integrated communications system that the instrument on his wrist will represent.

Energy consumption over a long period is expressed as Q. One Q unit is equal to 26 (American) billion tons of oil or 37 billion tons of coal: that is 10^{18}BTU. According to recent estimates, mankind consumed the equivalent of 6 to 9 Q from prehistoric times until 1850; 5 Q was consumed from 1850 to 1960. And from 1960 to 2060, it seems probable that some 100 Q will be consumed. This is one way of expressing, in materialist terms, the profound transformations that we are undergoing.

Nobody has measured the psychic energy consumed. That too must have increased dramatically (though on nothing like the scale of energy consumption), if only because of huge population growth.

Just as most of us live physically in environments that are essentially Victorian-with-burst-sides, so we live psychically in social environments that are outmoded. We have our spiritual Wandsworths. I have sketched one way in which the modern psyche could find a new social environment, away beyond the present mazes, through a radically altered educational system.

About every such utopian project, everyone is entitled to have their own reservations. I have one major reservation about my utopian project; I will state it and then I will have done.

18   M.E.R.O.'s Sinai Project, 1957–1970

Just how inevitable was the space race? Is it possible to think back to a time when the Americans and Russians might have turned instead to some other big project: for preference, not to nuclear war, but to the development of the Amazon Basin, or Siberia, say, on a really massive scale?

Events seem inevitable only after they have happened. As we have noticed, the space race appeared highly unlikely to almost everyone before the first sputniks went up. What of that ·00001 per cent for whom space-travel was a lifelong creed, Robert Goddard, Konstantin Tsiolkovsky, Hermann Oberth, and of course good old American Wernher von Braun? Plus, if you will, all the rabble of writers who supported their dreams with the lurid wish-fulfilments of *Planet Stories*. It may have been just an accident of history that things went their way.

One year before the first sputnik was launched in October 1956, the world-nightmare had reached new heights. There was revolution in Hungary against the oppression of Russian Communism; and British and French forces, acting in shameful collusion, bombed Egyptian airfields and started to invade Egypt, as old imperialist illusions of power, personified in the Prime Minister, Sir Anthony Eden, enjoyed a last fatal fling.

Just possibly, that folly could have been made a world-turning-point. As the British and French ignominiously withdrew, another ·000001 per cent might have risen up and been heard. Let us see what could have happened then. Let us suppose that U.N. Forces did more than take over in the Canal Zone. . . .

In addition to occupying the Canal Zone, the U.N. set up a new department, M.E.R.O., The Middle East Reclamation Organization. M.E.R.O. officials announced that the first practical steps would be taken to solve the hitherto intractable problem of the Middle East. Instead of selling arms to the rival Middle East nations, the Western Powers and their friends (and of course the Communist Bloc if it cared to join) would reclaim the melancholy wastes of the Sinai Desert, and the adjoining Negev Desert, apportioning the area reclaimed between the United Arab Republic, Jordan and Israel.

Israel immediately agreed to join in the M.E.R.O. project; her farmers were already raising bumper crops of wheat and barley in parts of the Negev. Russia, anxious to increase her influence in the area, exerted pressure on President Nasser, so that the U.A.R. also co-operated in the project. Anthony Eden headed for Jamaica.

The first M.E.R.O. task forces arrived on the fringes of the Sinai in February of 1957, a miscellaneous cohort of Swedes, Brazilians, Jugoslavs, Icelanders, Indians, Americans, Dutch, and two Norwegians. The World Press had an enjoyable time at their expense, especially when one of the Norwegians was shot by an itinerant Arab who hadn't heard that his world was going to be improved, and would not have liked it if he had.

'Promises to become an international ground-nuts affair,' commented *The Times* wryly, in a leader.

'Bring Eden Back!' bellowed the *Daily Express*.

But the work went on, and on, and gradually the cynics and idiots were—well, they were not silenced, but they began suddenly to praise the vision of a scheme which, they claimed, should have been commenced years earlier.

It was a costly enterprise. As the equipment piled up and the experts gathered, and the nuclear-powered desalination plants grew along the Mediterranean coast, astronomical sums were bandied about. The first twelve months alone were said to have cost £28.5 million (coincidentally, the cost of the American Survey 4 Moonprobe, written off as a failure).

Nor was the enterprise carried through without mistakes. Just before Christmas 1957, the great El Arish scandal blew up, as a result of which several eminent gentlemen lost their eminence. El Arish, the capital of the reclamation area, grew from a dozy Mediterranean port of some 11,000 people to a bustling city of almost a quarter million within a couple of years; it was only to be expected that rackets would be operating—as the leader of the Turko-Armenian gang pleaded when convicted for fiddling two million pounds worth of earth-shifting equipment and exporting it to Cyprus on a M.E.R.O. ship.

There was, too, the unfortunate case of the four hundred thousand eucalyptus trees, a gift from Australia, which were wrongly planted and not ringed with oil to preserve moisture, so that they perished.

These were minor setbacks, after all. The grasses began to grow over the dunes, the sisal plantations to spread. Thousands of sturdy acacias and eucalyptus saplings gave increasing shade to new highways. Desalination plants, powered by British nuclear reactors, began to spew forth almost drinkable water; a denazified German in Egyptian employ perfected a cheap solar-powered pump which would freshen as well as raise water. The Lussan dam began to generate hydro-electric power; pipelines cut the barren land into a uberous geometry. Meronized villages began to grow up here and there, each making its own impression on the desert; each had its varieties of specially developed maize, cane sugar, rice, cotton, and selected vegetables to grow in its new fields. The East–West system of canal, road and rail between Suez and Eilat on the Gulf of Aqaba began to extend inwards from both directions; near Nakhl El Tur, Dutch engineers struck oil.

For the industrial managers of the West, this oil find marked a turning point in their attitude to M.E.R.O. Though reluctantly, they were now convinced of its viability. Oil was to their superstitious minds what gold had been to their ancestors; they began to investigate (and invest in) the reviving area.

To the few local inhabitants of Nakhl El Tur, the oil was an incidental—at least at first, and until the full extent of the oil strata was realized.

The Nakhl El Tur oasis stands on the edge of true desert (or did until 1958, for it is now a strenuous market-city), beside an extensive dried-up salt lake. In the bad old days Nakhl grew little but dates, and even the date palms bore poor crops, owing to under-irrigation and lack of drainage. A three-man Dutch engineering team set themselves the limited objective of improving this position, after a U.N. doctor had reported on the high incidence of malnutritive diseases in the area. With solar-powered pumps, they watered the land, thus leaching residual salts out of the topsoil; at the same time, they lowered the water-table by drainage. They achieved their objective of doubling the date crop within three years. The discovery of oil was mere 'spin-off'.

This spin-off fostered side-effects of its own. As the rigs spread farther into the difficult terrain about Nakhl, the technologists on the spot found themselves in need of more adequate transport. So the first Tumvec ('tumbling vehicle') was developed, a crawler machine with tracks, which could engage its legs in crane-activity when necessary, striking its typical 'sit-up-and-beg' attitude. This machine was the predecessor of the tumvecs we today take for granted when they appear at the scene of an earthquake or similar disaster. No doubt they will be working on the lunar surface before long, and just as efficiently.

But the Nakhl tumvecs were clumsy and expensive. One-man machines were more suited to local conditions. So the Baliped came into service, the tall-walker that today in our cities often takes the place of automobiles and can be used by the aged and invalid, responding as it does to minute balancing movements by its operator. This machine has already changed the life of hundreds of thousands of people for the better.

The three Dutchmen of Nakhl were soon enlisted on a new project connected with the subterranean waters they had discovered. This was, of course, the construction of the world's first underground dam: seminal step towards the development of El Tur Science City, that peculiar blend of showmanship and high endeavour which still attracts so much popular attention today.

For anyone who has worked or lived in the fantastic underground environment of El Tur, this by-product of M.E.R.O. is the most interesting of all, and promises to lead farthest. The claims that its thirty-hour day is developing an 'anti-circadian man' may be poppycock, but El Tur's renowned 'freedom from day-night tyranny' has certainly led to the development of calescent behaviourism—which may, when more widely studied, alter our whole theory of the function of Man. Like hypnosis before it, calescent behaviourism is initially hard to credit—yet, in fifty years, we shall probably accept as a commonplace that man powers his own vehicles by a simple act of will.

Other so-called 'spin-off' bonuses appeared here and there in M.E.R.O. territory. Turquoise and manganese deposits were found, as well as subterranean lakes containing water from the Paleocene epoch, sixty million years old but perfectly drinkable, 1,750 feet down. Living in that water was a remarkable survival, a small fresh-water relation of the trilobite, the very existence of which had remained unsuspected and undetected; it survived in both bottom-dwelling and planktonic forms, to delight and puzzle the scientific world. More recent findings include the cave of a fifth-century anchorite in which was preserved a remarkable Codex of the late third or early fourth century, which throws new light on the relationship between Moses and Aaron, and the tribes of the Sinai.

By 1959, it had become the fashion to visit the Sinai Project. Student parties arrived from all over the world to give aid. Many stayed, to enjoy the life of dedication and adventure or to contribute to the populist movements developing in the area. Early agricultural schools expanded into colleges. The University of El Arish gained its charter in 1960, the University of Eilat in 1961. By then, the desert was blooming, yellow becoming brown and green, and of the 23,800 square miles involved in the project, almost one third lay under active reclamation.

From then on, progress was fast. Throughout the sixties, we have seen even more amazing developments. After no more than nineteen months wrangling, and the appearance of American and Russian fleets off the coast, Sinai declared itself an independent sovereign state, to be run jointly by Israelis and Arabs who rejoiced in declaring their common Semitic heritage. Its populist politics serve to give it an identity distinct from either of its immediate neighbours—between whom it is emerging as something more positive than a buffer state.

Independent Sinai has declared itself to be 'a warmer friendlier

Antarctica', open to science, its boundaries closed to no man. Its pleasure resorts have pioneered new perspectives in tourism. Its daring scheme for the damming of the southern end of the Red Sea and the reclamation of Saudi Arabia is now in stormy debate in the U.N. (whose investments in the area make it now a powerful para-national force to be reckoned with). But perhaps Sinai's most remarkable and impudent achievement was the announcement only last year of the Abolition of Passports Act. Sinai, Chile and Iceland are now the only countries one may enter without that offensive twentieth-century invention, the passport.

As for M.E.R.O., it was officially discontinued in 1969, but reconstituted under a new charter as T.W.A.R.O., the Third World Aid and Reclamation Organization. The new body has much wider powers, thanks chiefly to massive investments from giant corporations in U.S.A., U.S.S.R. and U.E. Under its stormy and able Chairman, Lord Ritchie-Calder, its charter enables it to draw 1·5 per cent of the G.N.P. from eleven contributory nations to ameliorate at last the complex socio-historico-economic problems resulting, at least in part, from the depredatory expansionist policies of European powers in Renaissance and Early Industrial eras. Unquote.

But this is no place in which to discuss the tentative solutions to the population explosion (perhaps the biggest problem mankind has ever surmounted); our concern is simply with the reclamation of the Sinai-Negev complex. However, it is worth remarking in passing that from those humble beginnings in February 1957 has flowed the present astonishing reawakening of hope in the West, the banishment of the old Cold War cynicism, with a concurrent decrease in mental illness and diminished crime rates, and the blossoming of the arts—led by Negro, Brazilian, Egyptian and Danish personalities. That simple creative act, the forming of M.E.R.O., has had consequences which have released a new epoch of human creativity.

For Independent Sinai itself, there is still a long way to go, and the initial project could hardly be termed complete; but the new Sinaiese development of inertial-flow control opens up dazzling prospects for world-transport, mechanical operations and space-travel; while the success of the whole project has encouraged other developing countries to invest money in similar reclamation projects (often supported by T.W.A.R.O.) rather than into high-prestige, low-yield projects such as national airlines, nuclear power stations, opera houses and independent deterrents.

The cost of all this has been beyond belief. Estimates put the figure at about $24,000 million (the cost of the space race to the United States of America between 1961 and 1969).

Britain in particular has been alarmed at such expenditure, and the newly proposed scheme to irrigate the entire Sahara has many critics.

'Bring Wilson Back!' pleads the *Daily Express*.

'Promises to become an international ground-nuts affair,' comments *The Times* wryly.

19   Conformity and the Everlasting Cornflake

Well, we know it didn't work out that way in reality. The money, the effort, the courage, the intellect, the discipline, the end result, went elsewhere: upwards into the wide blue yonder.

Space travel will bring its benefits (and to agriculture some of these benefits may come soon). But because it has gone ahead as it has, other projects no less rewarding in terms of prestige and returns have just never come up—I've pictured one of them, in the same sort of terms that chaps use to defend the space race.

My other picture, of super-communicating wards and fact-free education, will also fail to materialize, in all probability. One reason for this is political. For simplicity's sake, I have tried to leave politics out of the picture. Perhaps this is justifiable when we are talking about technology, the end product of research, for such technological wonders as the Concorde appear to get wished on us without proper political debate (even when they enjoy government subsidies); but research, pure science, is much more a subject for politics.

Politicians are of necessity short-sighted men. They are in

power for a brief term; they want quick results. For this reason, they are the less likely to back visionary schemes.

Times are particularly bad for politics in Western Europe. Caught between the two super-powers, we are in a little limbo of our own where the prospect of a United Europe, economically or politically, does not seem attainable or even very desirable (and if the super-powers did not find it desirable, they might be able to see that it was unattainable). So initiative is not with us. And our politicians are little men. I don't see any of them backing anything as visionary as my scheme for a new type of education.

The money, know-how, and all the rest that the scheme would require will probably be turned elsewhere: towards a manned flight to Mars, for instance. Back here on earth, we butterflies will continue to stifle in our nineteenth-century crysalises.

Let me explain why I believe the head will never give the heart a chance.

The youth of America were reported to be indifferent to the round-moon trip made by Lovell, Bowman and Anders before Christmas. Why? Because they sensed that this large-scale techno-logical circus was not for them, and was not run for their benefit. They did not share the middle-aged dream, and weren't going to be suckers. Young people in England feel more or less the same way about science. They prefer the arts. There's no progress in the arts, and it remains a sphere where the individual counts.

Technology is big money and big business—indeed, Big Business. And Big Business looks after itself, not people. Interests of producer and consumer are not identical.

When H. G. Wells was a lad, he saw how science could liberate him and thousands like him from the misery and circumscribed living of the lower-middle class. It did liberate him. But science was then somewhat of an outsider in its practical aspects; from being the pursuit of the Royal Society, it had become a left-wing activity—undermining the established order rather than support-ing it. Science was only just winning its battle against religion, which until then was king of the castle (Wells's revered teacher was Thomas Huxley, who spoke out at Oxford on Darwin's side against Bishop Wilberforce in the great debate on evolution).

Applied science has now climbed into the empty throne from which it deposed religion. It is in danger of becoming another tool in the hands of reactionaries, just as religion was in Victorian and Edwardian England. It could breed its own Royal Society.

There are many enlightened men who would not have it so; but, ever since politicians took control of the atomic bomb, the days when science was on the side of 'the little man' that Wells used to talk about have been numbered. From being an outsider, impure science has climbed to a position where it can have no time for the other outsiders. We are due for a new sovereignty that may prove more deadly than the last.

Think-tanks will help reinforce the new orthodoxy. They pre-determine increasingly how and where yet unborn millions will live, what they will eat, how large their rooms and cities shall be. What exists is possible: what is possible exists. The uniformity that best suits inflexible systems controlled by pre-planned pro-duction-lines and billion-dollar finance exists, is possible, and will exist. Pre-packaging can be forced upon consumer as upon consumer goods: in the interests of the economy, of course. If you want a picture of the future, think of a machine stuffing cornflakes into a human face—for ever!

Obviously such a rote-ruled system is never going to tolerate human beings with individuality and free minds, such as my modest educational proposal would encourage. Rote-ruled sys-tems need rote-ruled captives: stuffed full of enough facts between five and fifteen to enable them to work whatever machines still don't work themselves, and then crammed with all the fantasy the mass media can devise for the rest of their days!

That's the way it will go, most likely. Somewhere ahead, like a gap between fast-moving cloud through which one glimpses blue sky, is the gap in the production line of days which could bring greater psychic freedom to everyone alive: the education window. But trends are against us. When we get to the place where the gap was, we shall find it gone, non-existent, impossible, just as my 1957 Sinai project is non-existent and impossible.

We will find it gone. But we will be too busy to regret, if that's any consolation. For three men will be marching about on Mars, protected by spacesuits from the thin and bitter atmosphere, scuffing up a handful of grit in a self-operating shovel. Inside their armour, their three marvellous limbic brains will seethe with pride and delight—while three animal brains below will seethe with nightmare at what has happened to them. This fifty-yard amble on an alien planet will act as some distraction to the latest war-scare in the Middle East.

Stuck down here on Earth, all the rest of us will be able to see those three men over our super-communications systems. They will appear in colour and 3-D, life-size or little-finger size, at the turn of a knob. And we shall cheer madly, and our marvellous brains will seethe with pride and delight. Only deep inside, where we dream of larger achievements, will a small voice be screaming, 'Where does it switch off?'

The afternoon grows late. The moon is up already and the sun not down. I shall be able to be out after tea till dusk—half past six on such a fine day. With any luck, I can transplant a few more shrubs and carry on with the refencing of the field. Tomorrow is another day.

And there, but for a promise made some days and pages ago, I might be tempted to leave the matter. But pessimism is never a final answer; beyond it, there is always at least another question.

I promised to say something about Western civilization, and so I shall, knowing the folly of doing so. My excuse is that this whole book has already been on that topic, even if only indirectly. There has never been a greater civilization; nor can one imagine it being immediately replaced by anything but a long period of barbarism. Nevertheless, the signs are at present that it is, under its own impetus, heading towards a new technological barbarism, which I have tried to outline. The future offers none of the lightness and magic of Tiepolo; we are heading instead for one of Piranesi's prisons!

It is difficult to see what can be done to alleviate the position. To cry 'Wolf!' is not enough; many people have done that—I have enjoyed the exercise myself, for it is pleasurable playing the Cassandra role, in my novel *Earthworks*. If you get a field full of shepherds all crying 'Wolf!', the flocks die from lack of attention, if I may be allowed to mangle Aesop; but it can help to diagnose the position.

Underlying the magnificent diversity of our culture lies a fundamental question. Perhaps it is true to say that all civilizations are designed as answers to a fundamental question. The question changes, and is changed by men; then a different civilization, or a different facet of civilization, emerges.

Until not so long ago—until the Enlightenment, let's say—the fundamental question was, 'Is it God's Will?' And upon the resolution of that riddle was built much that we still hold to be worthwhile, including a great many of the things in the domain of architecture and the arts to which we accord our label Great.

But God went out of fashion, and his Will even more so. Among the agents of this notable change in life-orientation were such god-fearing men as Isaac Newton and Charles Darwin. Newton's new formulations in mathematics and physics paved the way for the Industrial Revolution and such researches as Carnot's attempts to determine mathematically 'how much work can be gotten out of a steam-engine', which led to the Laws of Thermodynamics. This new and independent spirit of inquiry led to a new question, 'To what extent can output be made to increase over input?' From this interest in a purely worldly efficiency has sprung the modern version of the question: 'Does it pay?'

We are uncannily successful. Our civilization is an ingenious answer to this question. By God, it does pay! The machine is buzzing at such a great rate that the trouble is over-production. True, much of the over-production is sunk in 'Defence'—which used to be known less politely as 'Armaments'—but even so we enjoy a cornucopia of benefits. Knocked sideways by the sight and sound of our success, all the other nations beyond the magic industrialized circle are clamouring for our secret formulae.

But there really are no secret formulae—only the underlying question, voiced often enough, one would have thought, for it to have become no secret. 'Does it pay?' Our current trouble is, we are now becoming sick of the question, which can only attend to the head and neglect the heart; the reality of it and its answer is wearing so thin that we sometimes appear to ourselves to be acting out a charade rather than the serious business of life. But how do you stop the machine now that it is going so fast and so well?

With all due deference to E. M. Forster and the gentle, privileged, old-fashioned school for whom he still seems able to speak, the answer is not to stop the machine. That way, we should die even more squalidly and more plentifully than under nuclear attack. The answer is to find a new question.

New questions do emerge. The decade of the sixties has provided a superficially attractive one: 'Does it feel good?' This, if I may be forgiven another reference to my own writings, is the question I attempted to answer in my novel *Barefoot in the Head*. To paraphrase, the answer would seem to be, 'No, because if everyone is preoccupied with trying to make themselves feel good, everyone feels bad.'

So the drop-out question 'Does it feel good?' is not generally valid enough. When the dominating question concerned God, there were always many who cared not a tinker's cuss for His Will. But it was a positive question, drawing forth a positive response. The drop-out question is essentially its reverse—'Is it My will?'—and as such is merely negative.

I can formulate a question to put forward that would immensely improve our present society without wrecking it, though I regard it only as a compromise, an interim riddle until—we hope—a genuine new life-giver emerges from the great sea-bed of mankind's psyche. My question would be: 'Does it make other people feel good as well?'

How naïve it looks, on paper! That war-abolisher, you will say, is an impossibly utopian question as yet.

To which I can merely bow my head in admission.

But if you agree that a peculiar powerlessness has gripped us just when we have acquired the Midas touch, if you agree that unease has caught us in the midst of unheard-of luxury, if you agree that politics can no longer solve even seemingly political matters, if you agree that the triumph of rationalism has brought with it a spate of unreason, if you agree that each fresh advance takes us deeper into the forest—in short, if you agree that head and heart no longer seem to have a body in common—then you must help towards framing tomorrow's fundamental question which will salve the unsatisfactory answers of today.

How should a human being live his life?

Does it make other people feel good as well?

Post-Lunar Postscript

Throughout this book, I took it for granted that I was writing in the year that men would set foot on the moon. They did so in the middle of July (a month ago, as I write this). It is one thing to anticipate an event, another to anticipate one's response to it—the swirl of adrenalin flushes some strange emotions.

In the succeeding month, the adrenalin has settled again, and it becomes hard to experience in retrospect the excitement of that day. They did it! They did it coolly and well, and in the achievement of the astronauts lies the answer to those sceptics who said the whole affair should have been left to machines.

Do we want machines to do our adventuring for us?

On that day, when one fifth of the human race watched Armstrong, Aldrin and Collins on television, my own scepticism was swept away. If much of it has returned, I now accept one fact of which I was unconvinced when I wrote this book: that the question of the Apollo project versus some great social project was never an either/or case. Good causes do not keep industry churning or production-graphs leaping.

Such reflections were far from me at the time of the actual moon-landing. As Margaret and I sat before the TV set, we could see the Moon through our wide windows, suspended apparently over the heads of the denizens of Stanford-in-the-Vale, and untarnished by the dulling afternoon air. Through powerful field-glasses, we could without trouble watch the Sea of Tranquillity.

I felt the landing through my system. Whatever one thought about its implications, there was the fact itself—something that I had believed would happen, had indeed held as an article of faith at a time when all the leading scientific authorities had poured scorn on the idea of space travel. As we stared at that ashen face, for so many ages and climates the property only of mankind's

fancies, we experienced the rare, rare frisson that comes when
entire systems of imagination come together, match velocities, and
coalesce into something new: when what was fantasy becomes
subject to the rigours of a return ticket.

At the beginning of that exciting week when the astronauts were
coming back to Earth and people who had never thought about
the implications of change and the future were forced to do so—
were glad to do so—I appeared on BBC's 'Panorama' to discuss
the value of the moon-landing with Professors Hugh Trevor-
Roper, George Porter and Barbara Ward. It was Barbara Ward
who convinced me that to say 'We must not go to the moon until
the black ghettos are eradicated' was as unproductive as wishing
that the money expended to equip Columbus for his voyages of
discovery had been lavished on Iberian hospitals to cure lepers.

For all that, there remains something about the moon fantasy
which causes alarm when one turns one's gaze to Earth. Although
it is true that alarmists in England were declaring her over-
populated in the twelfth century (as indeed she *was*, in terms of
the numbers of people the agricultural system could then support),
the alarmists eight centuries later must still make themselves
heard.

During that July week, I had the opportunity to sum up the
prospect as I saw it on the leader-page of the *Guardian*. This is
what I said.

'The first men on the moon are safely home, but all the hopes
and fears their voyage has started have still to settle down.

'Amid the uncertainties, a few facts are abundantly clear; new
sciences were born this week which as yet have no name, and new
currents in human history which have yet scarcely a formulation.
And yet; nothing has changed: man is still man. A few years ago,
it seemed a god-like thing to walk on another world; though we
know that beneath the space suits goes the parvenu neotenic ape,
species *homo sapiens*.

'It is in this Darwinian perspective that the implications of the
moon walk are best appreciated: a long perspective that can look
back and forward. It has taken mankind something like four
million generations to leave his planet. The dream has been there
for a long time, a descendant perhaps of the dream that propelled
fish out of the sea to walk on dry land, or apes out of trees to roam

the savannas. The technology to match the dream has come late.

'Man's progress, in fact, has been slow and uncertain. There have been centuries of stagnation, long periods of regression. For every Beethoven, Michelangelo or P. G. Wodehouse, history offers a profusion of Genghis Khans, Tamburlaines, Hitlers, and their lesser imitators. Christians have fought Christians, brothers killed brothers. Libraries have burned, knowledge has been lost, illusion has its perennial day.

'This somewhat dark view of history makes that moon walk seem so much the more marvellous—indeed, we are all fortunate to have survived to see it. In itself, the feat represents an immense achievement in terms of social organization, discipline, and planning ability which speaks well for the neotenic ape: which has never before performed with such prowess. But behind this great nuptial of modern skills lie two old basic attributes of the ape, tribalism and inquisitiveness.

'The inquisitiveness speaks for itself, though many may prefer the term "intellectual curiosity". As for the tribalism, NASA correctly stresses the scientific aspects of the Apollo mission, yet it remains true that the programme was launched by President Kennedy in 1961 with the object of outpacing the Russians in the space race; all other considerations remain subsidiary to this. In spite of which, science will benefit enormously.

'And so it ever was with man's enterprises. We are a divided species, head running ahead of heart; it is no surprise that coronary thrombosis is the characteristic death of our time—the heart literally chokes on the impossibility of keeping up. It is the neocortex that has powered man's evolutionary rise to domination over this small planet. Beneath the neocortex lies, unslumbering, the old animal brain.

'The fearful may hold that this latent schizophrenia in man will be aggravated by the moon walk. Success will breed success. The next project may be that much longer journey to Mars—possibly a twelve months' round trip. If excursions into space are triumphs for us all, equally they are triumphs for Big Business, and for the technology that goes hand in hand with Big Business. Will we be ruled by a technocracy? Will not technology become entrenched as a new religion, on the altars of which our humanity is sacrificed?

'At every stage such anxious questions arise. They represent in extreme form the ambivalence we feel towards our machines.

'In such areas of thought, we do well to doubt. Doubt is as contemporary as coherent light; where there are many possibilities, certainty is a form of blindness. What we can do is dismiss such questions as "Should the Apollo money have been spent on developing the underdeveloped countries or eradicating the black ghettoes?" The Apollo project is peaceful, and uses only 1 per cent of the American GNP. This form of question is better directed towards the Vietnam War; as it stands, it is on a par with the philistinism which asks why the National Gallery should spend a quarter of a million pounds buying a painting while there are still homeless in Battersea. Our world is not homogeneous. The poor are always with us: Botticellis and Apollos are birds of passage.

'It is true, nevertheless, that over-population with its attendant ills is a spectre at the moon feast. But we have not yet learned how to help a promising under-developed country like, say, Brazil, or a desperate one like, say, India, except through the fruits of science—and these will indeed accrue from our space activities. Much criticism of the space programme is covert sniping at the United States. That criticism is better directed at the USSR, which has not fulfilled an agricultural plan since 1929, and now imports millions of tons of grain from the United States. The Americans can afford to represent us in space; the Russian case is much less sound.

'So what is the future likely to bring? The next lunar landing is planned for November. Since 1961, many terrible things have happened to the Americans. We may take heart—and hope they also take heart—from NASA's declared intention to go ahead and explore the planets. This week's moon walk only makes sense when viewed in the light of such determination. It is significant that the prospect is outwards—to Mars and the planets beyond Mars, rather than to Venus and Mercury, the inner planets. Psychologically, this accords with our hopes rather than our fears.

'If the rivalry between the two great Powers continues, it is conceivable that Russia could over-spend herself and, by such commitments as buying increasing grain supplies from the States, fall under American influence. America herself might break—not merely through revolution, but through the collapse of essential services (as her telephone service is said to be creaking to a standstill while the company concerned pursues lucrative defence contracts). In that case, we may suppose that Asiatic races will become the inheritors of Space (but will a Scot be the first man to walk round the moon single-handed?).

'Personally, I believe that the old science fiction view of the future is more likely to eventuate. The possibility of a moon landing was an article of faith among SF-fans when all the scientists were crying "Twaddle!" It should be realized that in those same primitive breasts lies another article of faith, which is this: that man will explore and colonize the planets of his own system, and then reach out across the infinitudes of inter-stellar space seeking what the solar system lacks, new planets as beautiful as his own. These never-never lands will be reached either by exceeding the speed of light in some super-Einsteinian way (and Hoyle's latest theories allow us some hope on this score), or by shipping the passengers out in deep freeze, under care of a robot crew which will not suffer from a hundred-year voyage.

'What happens when neotenic ape reaches neotenic octopus, or neotenic dinosaur or neotenic ant, or whatever creatures may be assumed to share this galaxy with us, is beyond conjecture. We can only hope that our chaps behave as steadily as Armstrong, Aldrin and Collins.

'Such an encounter may lie no more than a century ahead. By then, the gallant lunar module will be seen for the quaint little Ford T model spaceship it is. By then, earth itself will be transformed as greatly as the last century has transformed it.

'With infinitely improved communication, miscegenation may have proceeded at such a pace that the majority of men and women enjoy the endurance of an Indian peasant, the industry of a Chinese, the friendliness of a Brazilian, the courage of a Yugoslav, the creativity of a Balinese, the independence of a Russian, the ingenuity of a Japanese, the self-questioning of an Englishman, the wealth of a Kuwaiti, and the sheer drive of an American.

'Out in the galaxy, all those abilities are going to be needed! Machines will also be needed. As they grow in ever-increasing numbers and refinement, so mankind must grow in stature to meet the challenge of his new environment. It will be ironic if heart and mind finally fall into step in another part of the galaxy: but growing up always entails leaving home.

'Perhaps it is only by setting many light years between ourselves and our planetary origins that we shall discover the most meaningful truths of the Universe within ourselves.'

This book is already a maze of themes; it is difficult not to respond with incoherence to the incoherent situation in which we find ourselves. We must accept that the complex world is a model of our own internal dynamisms.

It so happens that I write this postscript on the first anniversary of the Soviet invasion of Czechoslovakia, 21st August, three days after my birthday. In this peaceful country of England, it is hard to empathize with the Czechs, even now demonstrating in Wenceslas Square; yet their loss is, to a lesser degree, ours, for the brutal Soviet annihilation of Dubček's 'socialism with a human face' squashed a political alternative from which the rest of Europe could have benefited.

Had Dubček been permitted to go ahead and establish a Communist régime that permitted legal opposition and abolished censorship (something no other Communist party has dared to do), we might all have seen a new turning—a turning towards what I have called a new question. This would have had much more of a hopeful and liberating effect than a thousand men on the moon, a sign that the heart might synchronize with the head. It would have given new inspiration to many millions, inside and outside the frontiers of Communism.

It is hard to draw hope from the moon achievement, even if one views it from within the enclave of Caucasian privilege. For that achievement—a tremendous and formidable technological feat—is merely an extension of one of the trajectories of the past, and its space vehicle the utilitarian philosophy *in excelsis*, the steam engine *redivivus*, the latest bitter fruit of the Industrial Revolution.

The moon-landing, in other words, is a repetitive event, serving to remind us of the central problem that confronted intelligent men all last century: the fragmentation of society, with its corresponding isolation of the individual. This, together with other pressures, brought about the psychic distortions that we see epitomized alike in late Victorian hypocrisy and anxious contemporary hedonism, is reinforced by the moon-landing. No longer do we have merely—merely!—the Under-Developed and the Developed World. The United States has now become the Over-

Developed World. The world's store of envy and fragmentation has been increased.

This repetitive event extends the range of man's operations. It also confirms his inmost fantasies without satisfying them. One fifth of the world sat on its huckers and watched, via television, as Armstrong and Aldrin performed. But Armstrong and Aldrin were encased in their own little worlds: they breathed atmosphere imported from Earth; they wore napkins (diapers) like small children; they were precluded by layers of plastic and metal from actually touching the *terra nova* they had come so far, so uncomfortably, and so bravely, to inspect. Here was autism brought to perfection. Where, for God's sake, was reality?

Perhaps reality can only be retained on a personal level: one still retains custody of one's own head and heart. Voltaire's advice about cultivating one's garden remains good, limited though it is. Perhaps for this reason, the incumbents of Heath House continue to battle with the authorities for possession of our small field.

Although no headway has been made on this issue, headway has been made on the Evans-Newman theory of dreaming, and must be reported with pleasure here.

Just before the moon-landing, *Nature* published an article concerning an experimental test carried out in the States which seems to confirm the Evans-Newman hypothesis. Doctors Edmond Dewan and Ray Greenberg argued that if dreaming involved reprogramming processes, then victims of brain damage making good recoveries would show greater REM-activity than those making poor recoveries. They tested this idea on patients suffering from aphasia (loss of speech) in Boston Veterans Hospital.

When the experiment was completed, results showed that the good recoveries enjoyed over 20 per cent REM-sleep on average, while the poor recoveries enjoyed only 12·7 per cent. These results are consistent with the Evans-Newman theory.

Dewan and Greenberg are continuing with their researches.

Finally, let me quote from this week's *New Scientist*, in order that I may not be accused of bias against space travel.

New Scientist makes mention of Thor Heyerdahl's voyage in the papyrus boat, *Ra*, which took place at about the same time as Armstrong, Aldrin and Collins's more publicized voyage. Reporting to the UN, Heyerdahl says that large areas of the Atlantic—in mid-ocean as well as near the continental shores on both sides—are 'visibly polluted by human activity'.

The item continues: 'Even hundreds of miles from land, Heyerdahl and his crew were sailing through plastic bottles and other industrial garbage. What nauseated them most were what Heyerdahl described as sheets of "pelagic particles", samples of which he collected. The size of a pea, oily and sometimes encrusted with tiny particles, they smelt like a combination of rotting fish and raw sewage. Heyerdahl told a *Time* reporter that on five occasions he ran into patches of these particles so thick that the crew hesitated to dip their toothbrushes in the water, and once it was too dirty to wash the dishes in.'

So perhaps space travel will be presented with its glorious justification sooner than we imagine. The nations who are causing this unparalleled pollution of their world will soon have fouled it so much that they will no longer be able to tolerate conditions here. The President of the Over-Developed World, knee-deep in industrial garbage, will give the order. In fleet after fleet of space vehicles, the rich nations will blast off from Earth to fresh and sterile worlds: not just to the Moon but to Mars and the satellites of Jupiter, three of which are considerably larger than the Moon, and—even farther from the heat of the sun—to Titan and Japetus, both larger than the Moon, both satellites of the great and gaudy Saturn, ringed like a gipsy.

On those alien worlds, the benighted descendants of the Enlightenment will work out their unimaginable destiny. No longer bothered by the heart/head problem, for their hearts will be replaced at birth by prosthetic cardiac devices, they will indulge in marvels of technology, eventually replacing themselves by common consent by a more efficient race of animated computers.

As for poor old Earth. . . . As one prophet (not a science-fiction writer) said, the poor shall inherit it. . . .

Appendix 1

SLEEPING AND DREAMING—A NEW, 'FUNCTIONAL' THEORY
by Dr. Christopher Evans

Thanks to a series of ingenious and incisive experiments in recent years, we are now on the brink of a revolution—a revolution in our thinking about sleep and dreams. These experiments have provoked a theory that may enable us to explain, once and for all, why we sleep, why we dream, and why people need less sleep as they grow older. Because of these experiments, we may also be able to determine whether the psychoanalytic theory of dreams and sleep has any validity. Finally, we may even be in a position to answer that provocative question, Can we ever sleep less—recover part of the one third of our lives we spend sleeping?

Up to now, theories of sleep and dreams have fallen into three broad groups:

—the common-sense theory;
—the fantastical theory; and
—the psychoanalytic theory.

With the coming of the experimental findings of the past decade, a fourth theory has emerged, one we might call the 'functional' theory. Let us take up all four of them in order.

The most common-sense view of sleep is that it is a period of rest for both body and brain after the day's hectic activities. The support for this approach is obvious. First, physical activity clearly slows down during sleep. So, apparently, does mental activity, for sleep—except when 'disturbed' by dreams—seems to be a period of mental blankness, when thinking, learning, remembering, and so on come to a halt and the individual, for all practical purposes, ceases to exist. Second, after a 'sound' sleep we rise feeling refreshed, both physically and mentally. 'Rest' would seem

167

to be the prime cause. Dreams, by this view, are held to be weird intrusions into the sleep state, breakdowns in the brain's smooth rest cure, and they are to be avoided at all costs if a person is to get 'a good night's sleep'.

Unfortunately for this pleasingly simple hypothesis, there are some annoyingly contrary facts that have been around in one form or another for some decades and that give the common-sense view a bit of a knock. In the first place, it is simply not true that sleep is essential for bodily rest: the body's tissues are self-restoring and require relatively little inactivity. In fact, they function best when more or less continuously active, and need only brief periods of pause after persistent effort—the sort of pause achieved by an hour or so in an armchair. During sleep, in addition, there are regular periods of muscular movement specifically meant to *prevent* muscular inactivity.

As for the brain's resting, this might be a plausible hypothesis were it not for the interesting data from electroencephalography, data showing that, while there is a significant change in the *nature* of the EEG recordings during sleep (a shift towards the slower, high amplitude waves), there is no indication whatsoever that there is any *less* activity going on. Both of these are critical objections to the most commonly held view of sleep and dreams.

The popularity of the second theory, the fantastical, has declined somewhat in recent years (it is probably the oldest of the theories), but it is still very widely held, even if in a pseudo-sophisticated form. This theory is really a great set of sub-theories, all more or less plausible according to one's upbringing and inclinations, but at root all are manifestations of a single theme: During sleep, the soul or spirit is free to leave the body, and dreams are the soul's adventures during its free roaming. A modern variety of this—and one no less fantastic and no more scientific—is the version beloved by the Victorian psychical researcher and, in more restrained form, by the twentieth-century parapsychologist. Here the mind, during sleep, is in some strange way released from the shackles of the material world, and may either communicate 'telepathically' with other uninhibited minds, or receive special information about calamities of significance to the sleeper. Hence the portentous dreams of distant deaths and future events that make Myers and Gurney's *Phantasms of the Living* such a spine-tingling book, and that make up the bulk of J. W. Dunne's exercise in precognitive dreams, *An Experiment with Time*. (The latter is, incidentally, currently a paperback best seller in England.)

This theory is difficult to refute, but (personal preferences aside) much hinges, of course, on the general probability of the mind-body duality and of the existence of telepathy. The philosophical complications of the former have long been well known, while the scientific evidence for the latter, once considerable, now seems to be dwindling rapidly. We will not take this further here, but just suggest that this interesting theory now seems too far out of tune with the world, at least as we know it, to be any longer acceptable.

The most exciting and startling development in our understanding of sleep and dreams—until the very latest developments —has come from the Vienna school of psychoanalysis, and in particular from the tremendous insights of Sigmund Freud. Through the technique of free-association and the meticulous analysis of patients' dreams, Freud gradually became aware that dream content reflected (though often in weirdly distorted form) the individual's powerful emotional drives and conflicts. At first a hunch, this was soon built into the form of a theory which declared that dreams represented the pent-up emotional stresses and basic desires that the pressures of social conformity force us to repress or deny. In sleep, with the 'social censor' off guard, these repressed but still dynamic forces thrust to the surface as dreams. Hence the great importance attached by psychoanalysts, then and now, to the content of dreams as clues to a person's true personality.

This view of dreaming, with its extensive implications for theories of personality and motivation, and even for religious and moral beliefs, made relatively rapid headway in medico-scientific circles, although taking half a century to arouse more than jocular incredulity among lay people. But anyone who has spent any time at all pondering the content of his own dream-life will have little doubt about the validity of much of the psychoanalytic approach.

On the other hand, to all but the thoroughly indoctrinated, the gross deficiencies of the theory as a *comprehensive* approach will be obvious. To take the most glaring difficulty, what are we to make of those dreams, which we all experience at one time or another, that consist of simple, day-to-day happenings, quite clearly devoid of deep emotional significance? Psychoanalytic theory is well aware of this dangerous loophole, and has postulated a theory that dreams disguise their real meaning through bizarre distortions and cunningly planted red-herrings—the disguise being to prevent the startling nature of the repressed material from disturbing the dreamer's sleep and thus awakening him. This ingeniously gets over the criticism, but, alas, it lands psycho-analytic theory on the hook more firmly than ever—it forces the dream-interpreter into ever more desperate searches for deeply significant hidden meanings in totally innocuous dream material. The result has been that a slight air of levity, of the music-hall joke variety, has surrounded the relationship between the psycho-analyst and his interpretation of dreams.

Nevertheless, despite the drawbacks to the single-minded psychoanalytic theory of dreams, it is the theory that has remained undisputed master of the arena until recently.

In the late 1950's Dr. William Dement and colleagues at the Mount Sinai Hospital in New York began a series of experiments that were to have a more profound effect on the whole topic of sleep and dreams than any previous experimental approach. Dr. Dement and his co-workers had been taking a series of electro-physiological recordings of a subject's various activities during sleep. Apart from the generally familiar, if complex, EEG patterns, they also recorded the varying activity of a subject's eyes. In sleep, contrary to popular belief, the eyes are not rolled upwards, but in fact exhibit an extensive repertory of movements, some drifting and slow, others jerky and rapid, which take place at various intervals throughout the sleep period.

Of particular interest was the finding that when the subjects were awakened during one of these rapid eye-movement (REM) periods, they reported that they were—at the time of awakening—experiencing a dream. Surprise number two came when the amount of time devoted to dreaming (as measured by this new behavioural index) was counted up. Young adults, it was found, spent as much as 25 per cent of their sleeping time in REM-periods, and this percentage was even appreciably greater on certain occasions. Surprise number three, the biggest of all, had to await the publication in 1960 of Dr. Dement's now classic paper, *The Effect of Dream Deprivation.*

Dr. Dement had been quick to see that the extraordinary amount of time young adults spent dreaming suggested that dreaming had an important function. This possibility might be tested by depriving subjects of the opportunity to dream—by interrupting their REM-periods. His experiment, duly reported in *Science,* revealed that subjects deprived of REM-activity for several nights on end seemed to show behavioural or psychological disturbances. A control group, kept awake for an equal amount of time but *not* during REM-periods, remained, to all appearances, normal. Psychologists, psychiatrists and psychoanalysts all over the world pricked up their ears. Perhaps the real purpose of sleep was to allow us to *dream!*

Since then, Dr. Dement's experiment—with modifications— has been repeated in many laboratories, and its principal findings have not been effectively challenged. Subsequent experiments, in fact, strengthened the original idea. For example, it was found that subjects who had been deprived of REM-periods for some nights, when finally left to sleep normally, *spent a greater percentage of the sleep period in REM-activity than they did under normal conditions.* Enforced reduction in dreaming-time led to more dreaming in later sleep sessions.

These findings, which may be some of the most significant in the history of modern psychological research, seem to make it quite clear that sleep is *not* a period of rest or mental blankness, but a period designed to allow some kind of dynamic, and probably vital, process to take place. But what kind of process can this be?

The Computer Analogy

Pondering the function and nature of this process led a colleague, computer expert Ted Newman, and me to propose an analogy between dreaming and one type of computer activity. Let me explain. The more complex living brains seem to contain two repositories of memory—one short-term and the other more permanent. This is the 'dual memory-system' hypothesis. According to this hypothesis, events a person has experienced are first held in some labile system that has a high storage capacity but a restricted life. Then these events are accepted or rejected for long-term storage according to a built-in set of criteria. Events that pass the 'usefulness' test are then transferred to the permanent store. 'Rejects'—redundant material, erroneous actions—are totally disposed of, perhaps by the discharge of some kind of electrical circuit.

Now, for some time I had been trying to relate dreaming to the dual memory-system hypothesis. I had made no effort to work out the theory in detail, but it did seem to me that dreaming might correspond to the discharge of the short-term memory store. Dreaming might, in other words, be a way of rejecting useless memories. And when a dream is interrupted by the sleeper's awakening, it seemed to me, this would cause the dream to be 'experienced' and perhaps transferred to the permanent memory store. For this to be true, some form of scanning of the material held in the short-term store—a selection and classification procedure—must be taking place when a person dreams. As it stood, the theory, if one can call it that, was little better than a slightly more up-to-date version of the 'dreams as mental defecation' idea, which is quite venerable in one form or another. An important insight, however, came after Newman and I had been discussing certain activities of advanced and complex computers.

Computers perform a variety of complex tasks according to a set of programmes—instruction to the machine to use its analytic equipment in a certain way. As computers develop in size and complexity, and as the range of tasks for which they are equipped increases, it becomes gradually more important for the programmes to be regularly revised and reclassified—in order to bring the computer up to date. Take computers that control the wage and salary system for a large firm. As wages increase, taxes change and the size of the payroll varies. So the computer's programmes must constantly be altered. Now, as things stand with today's relatively simple-minded computers, this programme-clearance may be done by a technician. He takes the computer 'off-line' (uncouples it from the task it is controlling), then runs the programmes through and makes modifications where necessary. In order to perform this set of operations, it is imperative that the computer be off-line. Otherwise, the experimental or modified programmes will do the job they were intended to do *as they are being run through*. So, if there is an error in the programme, we would get sets of peculiar pay-checks coming up at the wrong time, or worse, if the computer were controlling operations in some form of chemical factory, disastrous explosions might result.

Our brain-computer analogy states that the purpose of sleep is to take a man's brain 'off-line'—to prepare for revising and clearing the brain's programmes in the light of recent events and experiences. Dreaming, by this analogy, is the *running-through of the programmes and their reclassifications*. Yet we normally are not aware of this clearance of experiences. Only when the process is interrupted, because of some external or internal disturbance of the sleeper, will consciousness interact with the clearance activity, *and what we popularly call a dream* be experienced. A dream is thus either a useful or a useless experience that is being classified.

In short, sleep is a process *intended* to allow us to dream, and to dream without interruption from the external world (which might muddle-up existing programmes) and without the programme-clearance operation interacting with the world in a positive fashion (we are not, unfortunately, completely 'off-line' when we sleep-talk or sleep-walk).

The content of most dreams, incidentally, is probably trivial, since most of our experiences are of the useless variety. At first thought, this seems to conflict with one's own subjective impressions. The apparent significance of much of our dreaming can be understood, however, when we remember that we are talking about *interrupted* dreams in this context, and it is dreams with great *effect*, and provoking autonomic bodily reactions, that are most likely to wake us up. The vast bulk of undisturbed dreaming, in fact, will probably consist of very drab, routine material—the bread-and-butter experiences of the previous day being fitted into the programme system. Occasionally we become aware of this boring rubbish when a fever brings fitful sleep. Then we see the core of dreams for what they really are: endless sessions of counting; reading nonsense; attempts to solve weird problems; driving vast distances; and so on. To slightly misquote an acknowledged expert on the topic, this is really 'the stuff of dreams', and we should be very glad that we normally sleep through it all.

Explaining Hallucinations

What might be the effect of interfering persistently with this memory-clearing activity? Computers whose programmes are not modified regularly get progressively less and less efficient at their jobs, and programmes could become badly muddled if classification processes broke down. Humans, when deprived of sleep, and therefore of dreaming, become muddled and confused, and soon find all but the simplest of tasks difficult. In due course, there may be psychotic episodes, and hallucinations (emergency waking dreams?) may appear.

We may be a long way from computers hallucinating, but one can easily imagine that some form of automatic programme-clearance system might usefully be built into the very complex and comprehensive computers of the not-too-distant future. Those of us who are of a fanciful turn of mind might like to call *this* dreaming.

Dr. Dement's exciting and original experiments, in addition to provoking this 'functional' theory of sleep and dreams, also oblige us to change our view of that third portion of our lives that we had considered to be empty and lost. Thus, a recent science-fiction novel, and more than one short story, has had as its theme the possibility of reclaiming the sleeping hours. This kind of speculation no longer makes sense now, and suggests that an important change in attitude may be necessary. One obvious example comes to mind. If the programme-clearance analogy is a good one, then we should expect significant differences in sleep (dream) requirements with age. *New* material affects existing programmes the most, and in youth, when our sensory-gathering equipment is at the peak of its efficiency and our ability to learn is the greatest, we will therefore require the most sleep. With old age, and its obvious concomitants, sleep requirements should drastically fall off. Old people, then, should be taught to accept their lack of need for sleep and, where possible, learn to enjoy the hours they have gradually regained.

A second change of attitude that may be necessary concerns our use of drugs. The level of sleep needed for 'good dreaming' to take place might be quite precise, and one can imagine that certain drugs might well depress the individual *below* this level. One might therefore 'sleep like a log' but in fact be no better off, in the important sense, as the result of the sleep. (Recent experiments by Jouvet in France indicate that the REM-phase *is* inhibited by barbiturates.) Conversely, hallucinogenic drugs, including LSD in its various forms, might produce their effects by activating the dream-mechanism at unsuitable times—in particular, when the brain is not off-line. The dangers of permanent interference with the dreaming process could be great, and the hallucinogens might be fearfully risky to play with.

Finally, as far as this article is concerned, what are we now to think of psychoanalytic theories of dreams? Curiously, in an important way, it seems to me that psychoanalytic theory is helped rather than hindered—because the analyst is relieved of the need to observe or uncover significance in every remembered dream. Dreams of emotional and psychoanalytic importance will, of course, still occur, their frequency depending on the role that their subject matter plays in the patient's waking life. They will be just as revealing to dream-analysis. But the good analyst, however, will now need to learn to distinguish between the genuinely significant and the genuinely trivial in the individual's dream life.

(Reprinted from *Trans-action*, December 1967)

Appendix 2

FRAGMENTATION OF PATTERNED TARGETS WHEN VIEWED AS PROLONGED AFTER-IMAGES (Reprinted from *Nature*, No. 1. 199, No. 4899 21 September, 1963)

When an object is viewed through some optical system which stabilizes its image on the retina a breakdown of normal vision occurs and the target may disappear.[1], [2] When complex targets are viewed under these conditions disappearances may be partial,[3] and the fragmentations which occur may consist of distinctly ordered, non-random segments of the original figure.[4]

Most workers (for example, see refs. 5 and 6) observe, with their stabilizing apparatus, that targets disappear and reappear at short intervals when viewed for several minutes. Sometimes the whole and sometimes part of the target reappears.[3] One worker[7] suggests that all reappearances are due to a failure of the stabilization system through slippage of a contact lens, but it is difficult to explain partial reappearances in this way. Slippage would cause the entire image to shift across the retina and fall on fresh receptors. The question would be clarified if complete stabilization, without possibility of movement of the retinal image, could be achieved. It is indisputably difficult to eliminate slip of a contact lens[7] and impossible to prove that this has been done, but after-images are almost certainly stationary on the retina.[8-10]

In the present experiment we investigated the appearance of prolonged, patterned after-images. The experimental targets were drawn up on black paper out of which the outline shape of the required pattern could be cut. The black paper was backed with a sheet of tracing paper. The target was illuminated from behind by a photographic flash-bulb set in a reflector. The translucent parts of the target appeared very bright, yet evenly illuminated. With Philips 'PF5' bulbs in a 7-in. reflector, the after-image

176

remained visible for at least 10 min., and was sufficiently clear and positive to allow unequivocal observations to be made for at least 5 min. The duration of the flash (maker's tables) was 24 m.sec. and the duration above half-peak intensity 12 m.sec. The estimated brightness of the target was about 10^6 candles m.$^{-2}$ sec.

Five subjects were presented with the target simultaneously. Each stood about 3 m. from the target, which, 10 cm. in diameter, subtended an angle of approximately 2 degrees. Subjects were each instructed to fixate a particular point on the target with one eye covered. Directly the flash had occurred the experimenter switched out the lights, leaving the room in complete darkness.

After 5 min. observation under these conditions, subjects were asked to report on the phenomena that had occurred. Further trials were conducted after a period of at least 15 min. had elapsed. Observations from trial to trial were made with alternate eyes.

The targets used were those illustrated in Fig. 1. Two trials were made with each target and all subjects reported sharp and definite after-images in each case. The general nature of the results may be summarized as follows: (a) After-images were of great clarity and brilliance initially, gradually losing detail but retaining sufficient positive qualities to allow reasonable observations to be made for the experimental period. (b) After-images faded frequently but at unpredictable intervals. Fading or disappearance was occasionally of the complete pattern, but more commonly of some part or parts of it. (c) There was a strong tendency for the straight lines of which a target was composed to fade as units. Typical fragmentation effects for Fig. 1C are illustrated in Fig. 2. (d) After fading, the image would reappear after some indefinite period of time. The nature of its reappearance was often total, that is, the image would regenerate to its normal state as a complete pattern. All subjects also reported that partial regenerations of the image might occur, and that these might feature the reappearance of single or parallel straight lines as units. (e) The segment of the target least likely to disappear was in the neighbourhood of the fixation point; the more peripheral the part of the pattern, the more likely it was to disappear. (f) After about 3 min., subjects reported a tendency for filling in of the whole of the enclosed part of the target. In due course detail was found to reappear in full. Similar results have been obtained with stabilized retinal images.[5]

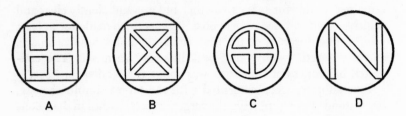

FIG. 1. Targets used in the study. The side of the square
subtended 2° arc

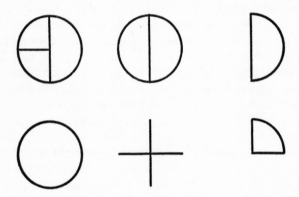

FIG. 2. Diagram showing the most frequent fragmentations
observed with the after-image. It will be noted that entire figures
are typical

It has been found that, with vivid after-images of geometrical
outline shapes, a range of disappearance and reappearance phenomena is experienced comparable with that reported from studies
utilizing mechanical stabilizing systems. Of particular interest is
the finding that disappearances may be structured, and that a
large number of reappearance effects are only partial.

Yarbus[11] and Barlow[7] have suggested that a perfectly stabilized
image will suffer total and lasting disappearance and that regeneration of the image must be a consequence of mechanical lens
destabilization. While it is not disputed that contact lens slip will
induce reappearance of an image, it now seems most likely that the
partial and structured reappearances of images reported in this and
other[3] studies cannot be attributed solely to such movement.

Theories of retinal function that predict permanent disappearance of stabilized images will therefore need reconsideration.

This investigation was supported in whole by Public Health Service grant No. NB. 01233–07, from the U.S. Department of Health, Education and Welfare.

H. C. Bennet-Clark*
C. R. Evans

Department of Physics,
University of Reading

References

1. Ditchburn, R. W. and Fender, D. H., *Optica Acta*, 2, 128 (1955).
2. Riggs, L. A., Ratliff, F., Cornsweet, J. C. and Cornsweet, T. N., *J. Opt. Soc. Amer.*, 43, 495 (1953).
3. Pritchard, R. M., Heron, W. and Hebb, D. O., *Canad. J. Psychol.*, 14, 67 (1960).
4. Pritchard, R. M., *Sci. Amer.*, 204, 72 (1961).
5. Evans, C. R. (in preparation).
6. Hebb, D. O., *Amer. Psychol.*, 18, 16 (1963).
7. Barlow, H. B., *Quart. J. Exp. Psychol.*, 15, 36 (1963).
8. Craik, K. J. W., *Nature*, 145, 512 (1940).
9. Brindley, G. S., *J. Physiol.*, 147, 194 (1959).
10. Brindley, G. S., *J. Physiol.*, 164, 168 (1962).
11. Yarbus, A. L., *Biophysics*, 2, 683 (1957).

* Present address: Department of Zoology, The University, Edinburgh,

Appendix 3

AUDITORY 'STABILIZED IMAGES'; FRAGMENTATION AND DISTORTION OF WORDS WITH REPEATED PRESENTATION by Dr C. R. Evans, Miss M Longdon, E. A. Newman and B. E. Pay.

Reproduced by permission of the Director, National Physical Laboratory.

When patterns are stabilized on the retina by one method or another[1] [2] [3] perception fails and striking fragmentation effects occur. In brief, patterns break up into non-random segments of which the most characteristic are straight lines; a pattern such as a circle with an inscribed cross, for example, will typically lose either the vertical or the horizontal bar, or the whole cross, or occasionally the whole circle leaving the cross intact. Regeneration of the pattern either in whole or in part occurs from time to time. These effects are reliably reported by all subjects viewing patterns as stabilized retinal images, the basic units being the same for all observers, though the sequence and rate of change may vary appreciably.

It has been suggested[4] that the fragmenting units may imply the existence in the human visual system of a classificatory pattern recognition mechanism similar in principle to that apparently present in the cat's visual cortex.[5] Using this as a working hypothesis we are currently engaged in a study of stabilization phenomena in an attempt to determine the basic human classificatory units to assist us in the logical problems of the design and construction of pattern recognition machines. Some of our results[6] seem sufficiently promising to make us eager to consider the possibility of providing auditory 'stabilized images' to help us in parallel studies of auditory perception and the design of speech recognition machines.

Now contact lenses with tiny targets attached to them[3] [4] or very bright flashes of short duration[6] may provide visually stabilized images, but these are *spatially stabilized*, and clearly there can be no durable analogue for this in the auditory system. The essence of the matter, however, seems to be not so much restriction of movement on the retina, but rather a lack of significant change in the nature of the input. If this is so, then rapid and extended repetition of sounds and words producing *temporal* rather than *spatial* invariance should bring about some form of failure of auditory perception.

With this argument in mind, and being aware of the common observation that a word repeated aloud to oneself a number of times soon becomes curiously lacking in meaning, we set out to test this hypothesis, and in doing so unwittingly 'rediscovered' an effect first noted apparently by Warren and Gregory[7] and later reported in some detail by Warren.[8] Our findings offer complete confirmation of the Warren-Gregory effect, and for this reason we will present them only in summary. Fifty subjects heard words played to them through earphones, the stimulus word being repeated approximately 40 times per minute from an endless-loop tape. Four words, BAG, SNOOL, KETTLE and DOBERMAN were used and in any one run, of course, subjects heard only one of these four words. Subjects were given pencil and paper and instructed to write down any sounds or combinations of sounds, whether meaningful or nonsense, which they heard in the course of the run. The volume control of the tape-recorder was turned up until subjects reported it to be 'unpleasantly loud', after which it was turned down fractionally. Words were repeated for periods of 5, 10 or 15 minutes. A few selected subjects listened for one-hour periods. Phenomena reported were very striking and could be divided broadly into two classes, (a) fragmentation and (b) distortion. By (a) fragmentation we refer to occasions when some part or parts of a word became lost, the core of the word, however, remaining unaltered; 29 out of 50 subjects reported this phenomenon. Distortions (b) were experienced by all subjects with varying frequency, and were often of a dramatic and, occasionally, disturbing nature. The over-riding impression was as if a new word had been substituted on the tape or had intruded itself into the sequence, and this in fact is what the majority of subjects were convinced had happened. Even the experimenters themselves when acting as subjects occasionally found it hard to believe that only one word was being played. As Warren has reported, most substitute words bore some obvious relationship to the originals; KETTLE for example frequently became PETAL, TATTLE, and even on one occasion CATALOGUE. Vowel distortions were slightly more common than consonant distortions though both occurred very readily; the word BAG for example often became EIGER or TIGER. Table 1 shows a variety of common phantom words reported for each original.

By a conscious effort it was usually possible to 'bring back' the basic word when a phantom word was being heard; however, this facility seemed to wane markedly as the length of the session wore on. Most subjects taking part in 15-minute sessions found that the original word rarely reappeared and then seldom at will. Individual phantom words might persist for minutes on end, being heard therefore for literally hundreds of times, during which time the subject had ample opportunity to assure himself of their objectivity. This was true even for those subjects who realized at some stage in the proceedings that one word only must be being played. The phantom word might persist even when the subject 'thought' of the original, read it, spoke it or wrote it down.

It is important to convey the fact that the distorted words have a very 'real' sound—even to subjects who know that they are only being fed a single physically unchanging stimulus. The fact that phantom words seem virtually indistinguishable from the 'real' ones suggests that the basic neurological response itself is changed, and that the complex which normally mediates the perception of a particular word is no longer capable of firing. Thus the system obliged to respond in some way to the continuing input produces an 'incorrect' but partially acceptable alternative.

To anyone who, like the authors, has experienced the striking fragmentation effects and perceptual changes occurring in the visual field when patterns are stabilized on the retina, it is tempting to propose a logical link between the two sets of phenomena in the different modalities. The link may appear tenuous, but if it can be accepted, the phenomena of auditory change make more sense than they seemed likely to do when first reported.

The work described above has been carried out as part of the research programme of the National Physical Laboratory.

C. R. Evans
M. Longden
E. A. Newman
B. E. Pay

References

1. Ditchburn, R. W. and Pritchard, R. M., *Nature*, 177, 434 (1956).
2. Evans, C. R. and Piggins, D. J., *Brit. J. Physiol. Optics*, 20, 1 (1963).
3. Bennet-Clark, H. C. and Evans, C. R., *Nature*, 199, 1,215 (1963).
4. Evans, C. R., *Brit. J. Psychol.*, 56, 2 & 3, 121 (1965).
5. Hubel, D. H. and Weisel, T. N., *J. Physiol.*, 160, 106 (1962).
6. Evans, C. R., *Brit. J. Psychol.* (in the press).
7. Warren, R. M. and Gregory, R. L., *Amer. J. Psychol.*, 71, 612 (1958).
8. Warren, R. M., *Brit. J. Psychol.*, 52, 3, 249 (1961).

Table One

Bag	Snool	Kettle	Doberman
BIGGER	SNOW	PETAL	PAPERMAN
EIGER	SNORE	PEBBLE	PEPPERMINT
ADA	SMALL	TITTLE	PERGAMON
ELEGANT	SNOWBALL	TALKIE	PLATINUM
BED	KNOW-ALL	CATALOGUE	TWICKENHAM

Table 1: Examples of some 'phantom' words reported by various subjects.

Appendix 4

DESTABLIZED VERSIONS OF TWO POEMS See page 78

It is possible that if the prescriptions were followed, the fragmentation and distortion process would become reversed in such a way that the following original poems would remerge. (Or perhaps entirely new 'in-built' poems might emerge.)

I. Sensory Deprivation

In the garden the snow lies
  Cozened by wall and hedge
Deep under winter's sta-
  bilizing hand

Bare's the table empty's the plate
  Of my green intentions
All's in numb suspense
  While icicles drip

II. Conference Tables

Outside reporters
Clutch microphones
Trying to dramatize
Minor issues

Inside politicians
Play the Great Game
Trying to gloss over
Major issues

Appendix 5

As on the first day at first
There is hope in writing
Light dividing from darkness
And a mighty heave of heart
At first sight of the stage

Filled all too soon with creeping things
Intended for your benefit and mine
To fly   Let the analogy
Fade   For more than seven days
I laboured into my history

I still do battle
You still embrace
Your intricate fields
Idols and engines
Unaware how I bleed

All I can hope is
I'll raise a slow-flowering war
And lie in you like the dead
Under hawthorn hedges
After Agincourt